CONVERSATIONS

WITH

André Gide

CONVERSATIONS
WITH
André Gide

BY

Claude Mauriac

TRANSLATED FROM THE FRENCH BY

MICHAEL LEBECK

George Braziller

NEW YORK

To my father
whose testimony
here answers that
of André Gide

Contents

Introduction

In France, writers are stars. In addition to publishing their books, they are encouraged to play roles. An alert, cultivated public takes them seriously. As long as they hold the stage, it follows their progress, cheering them on, and when they die, it not only mourns them in special issues of half a dozen weeklies devoted to the arts, it remembers them, retelling, sometimes even inventing characteristic stories about them. Thus the week André Gide died, in February 1951, the text of a telegram appeared on a bulletin board in the halls of the Sorbonne. How it got there was a mystery, but it was signed Gide, and it read as follows: *"L'enfer n'existe pas. Previens Claudel."* "Hell doesn't exist. Better warn Claudel."

It was what we call an "in" joke; yet in France the community for such a joke included a vast general public as well as students and journalists. For generations, Gide and Claudel had been two of the brightest stars in the literary heavens. While both were still living, their correspondence had been published, and their half-century quarrel had become meaningful public property, a living allegory, comparable to what Olympian myths must have been for the early Greeks.

Massively self-assured, Claudel had stood for not only

Catholicism, but for the man whose belief is not a matter of being intellectually convinced, the man for whom faith is itself a mode of prehension, separate and not dependent upon the reasoning faculties. To this point of view, Gide had opposed not the mere atheism Sartre credited him with, but his temperamental elusiveness, his obstinate and very French instinct to remain free, self-questioning, self-sufficing, self-reviewing, as individual as possible. For years, Claudel had been sympathetic, trying first to persuade, then to bully, finally to admonish Gide into choosing his own orthodoxy. But Gide remained tentative. He came close. He seemed to nibble. But then he escaped, true only to his own nature, going on to other possibilities, while Claudel fiercely dismissed him as only "a man fascinated by mirrors." The myth proliferated. One story told of Claudel holding up a flaming *crêpe suzette* at a dinner party and exclaiming, "That's how Gide will burn in hell!" A sequel told how a young man present at the same party had come to Gide and said, "Now I know who is the real Christian."

And so on. The point is that for decades Gide and Claudel, among others, served the literate community of France in something like a sacerdotal capacity. They were living emblems as well as authors. They carried the drama of their personal experience—seasoned, of course, with a sense of theater—out into the public world and enacted much of it there, and all as part of a serious, civilized game for serious, civilized people.

In England, or here in America, we seem to be embarrassed by this sort of thing. We draw a line between a writer's work, on the one hand, and his private life, beliefs, and actions, on the other, and we insist that only the former are of any concern to us. But the truth is, we are simply not very interested in anything to do with literature. Neither as art nor as testament is it a part of our community life. We do not take it seriously. We are not impassioned by its risks or revelations. We read for relief, and at most, we will allow an author to murmur easy generalities. If he ventures particulars, we are uncomfortable. If they are particulars about himself, about what he could have known or been, we are usually distressed.

Perhaps it is because the French love their language, and therefore, anyone who uses it with glamour or distinction. Perhaps it is because, more than any other people, they revere a maximum of individuality, and therefore the writer whose books struggle to define his own. Perhaps, over the centuries, they have simply led less psychologically sheltered and morally timorous lives than the rest of us, and therefore more urgently need to know some of the truth about themselves before they die. In any case, they are not afraid of their writers. They cherish and believe in them—and not just as we believe in film stars and waifs who grow up to make a million dollars.

Without any loss of dignity, a writer in France may come to embody something; nothing necessarily doctrinaire, but something succinct all the same: a way of life, a temperament, a style. Colette, for example, was not only a novelist, but the pantheon example of certain French ideals of taste, conduct, and earthly fulfillment. To thousands of readers to whom her vocabulary and syntax may have been difficult, she nevertheless represented gourmandise, self-control, *mesure*—above all, a manner of living for seven or eight decades on the earth with dignity.

It has been the same with Valéry, Cocteau, François

Mauriac; with Montherlant, Julien Green, Marcel Jouhandeau; with Camus, Sartre, Jean Genet. But of all these stars of the twentieth century, none lent his personal history to public use more resourcefully than André Gide. *"Ne me comprennez si vite,"* he said. "Don't be too quick to understand me." Gide himself took eighty years, annotating all the way, in novels, plays, essays, and his journal. It is not enough to say he was honest. He had a manifold nature—though perhaps no more manifold than many people's; what made him exceptional was the persistence and courage with which he explored, and used, and recorded his variety. He was intellectual and sensual and taught himself to nourish both of these appetites. In the course of his life, he tried Marx as well as Christ; he loved men as well as women; he married, had a child, became a grandfather; he cultivated great friendships and suffered unrequited love; he played the piano, seduced boys, learned Latin and English and German; he wrote books on such extra-literary subjects as jury-duty, Chopin, the Congo, Soviet Russia; and in all these relations and activities, he was a scrupulous and responsible star.

A book like Claude Mauriac's *Conversations with André Gide* presupposes this kind of stardom. It also presupposes a reader who is game. If, for instance, you think the diary form itself is an indiscretion, or that any public use of private lives is indecorous, or that literature is *only* a safe, disinterested form of "superior amusement," then you had probably better bypass this book, just as you had better bypass much of French literature from Villon and Montaigne on. But if you are not that shy, if you can trust a

xii

writer enough to let him be intimate, then this journal will be a refreshing, often hilarious, always nutritious experience.

First, though, a few details of background and dramatis personae may be in order. Like any authentic diary, these pages were written on the spot, from day to day. They may have been emended or trimmed. But they remain excerpts from a diary, written for the author's own sake, with references and loose ends which may not be familiar even to French readers.

The story begins one October evening in 1937. The diarist is twenty-three, and the son of François Mauriac, the most distinguished Catholic novelist of his generation in France. Young Claude has been, so to speak, bred to the literary vocation, and he is already writing a book about another Catholic novelist, Marcel Jouhandeau. Then, sitting in a restaurant one evening, he recognizes André Gide at an adjacent table. He has never been introduced to the great man, but hero-worshiper that he is, he cannot miss the chance. He stands up, walks over, and presents himself.

At this point in his life, Gide was at a crest of more than literary notoriety. He had been famous, or infamous, since the early Twenties, but as a sexual moralist, having been the first man of letters in world literature to make explicit and reasoned claims for the place of homosexual experience in human life. Great writers had written out of homosexual experience before, from Sappho to Shakespeare to Proust. But no serious literary artist had asked the world, in so many words, to regard homosexuality as simply another given fact in mankind's possibilities. Gide had done this in *Corydon,* and throughout the Twenties, he was either praised as a liberator, or damned as a corruptor.

In the Thirties, things changed. The young people whom Gide's example, among others, had influenced, were older now, and having perhaps liberated their private lives in some degree, they were now asking themselves what could be done about their community. Gide himself became more and more interested in political action. As early as 1928, he had published a courageous exposure of French colonial abuses in the Congo. And though, like *Corydon,* it may seem very obvious now, no comparably important writer was saying it at the time.

The same was to be true of his books about Soviet Russia. In 1936, after a suitable period of mutual flirtation, Gide was invited to Moscow, and there, standing beside Stalin on Red Square, he delivered a speech at the funeral of Gorki. He toured the country until September, and when he returned to France, he was oppressed by the conviction that revolution, in the name of greater liberty, had only engendered greater constriction of individual life and thought.

Courageous again, he published two books about what he had seen, and they aroused the organized fury of not only the world-wide Communist Party, but the righteous indignation of liberals everywhere. At the same time, they brought Gide the mixed blessing of right-wing sympathy, in particular, a generous acknowledgment from Mauriac *père.* But it left Gide himself, at sixty-eight, very much alone, and it was in this troubled state of mind that he first looked up and saw young Claude.

Their subsequent encounters were well-meaning, but

Gide's life was complex. He left Paris soon after, and the following spring, in 1938, his wife died, precipitating an extreme personal crisis of loneliness and guilt. That winter he went to Greece, describing himself as *"libre effroyablement,"* "dreadfully free," and it is the following May, in 1939, that Claude's story really gets under way. Gide is invited to visit the Mauriac estate near Bordeaux, and the close account of these days—as well as the later August weeks in Pontigny—gives us something of the same sense of human life, human mystery, which we get from a good novel.

Speaking of novels, Glenway Wescott once pointed out that their "incident, description, characterization, dialogue, are the means of expression of truths that are greater, more affecting, than anything that can be put in general or theoretical form." A diary, in this respect, can be as satisfying as a novel, and certain scenes in these *Conversations* seem to me as graphic, memorable, and iridescent with truth as anything—let me be precise—which I have found in Gide's own novels, or Mauriac *père*'s, or those Claude himself has since published. For instance, the scene (May 23, 1939) in which Gide, facing a sympathetic stranger, tries to find words for the as yet tentative stage of their relationship, to admit his own hopes for it, to reassure the shyness each is impaled on; or the scene (July 3, 1939)—funny, cruel, touching, and much more— in which Mauriac *père* sees Gide off on an afternoon walk; or the numerous scenes in which Mauriac and Gide sit like two Olympic gods, gravely, candidly tallying up Gide's failures and hopes. Only certain pages in the novels of Henry Green have ever given me so poignant a sense of how needfully human beings struggle to communicate with each other, and of how little, in the last analysis, even the most articulate of us can actually tell, how little we can be of *use* to each other.

Then there is also the "stardust" value of the book: shrill and dazzling Cocteau exhausting his entourage with an all-night monologue in his Versailles hotel room; brusque Colette, thrusting Cocteau before a mirror and assuring him that she never wants to be as skinny as he is; Laurence Olivier, almost naked in his dressing room, and coldly receiving Gide without realizing who he is; Valéry on his deathbed; and best, or most bizarre, of all, the dinner with Marcel and Elise Jouhandeau.

Of his contemporaries, Jouhandeau (born 1888) is easily the most original living writer in France, and though he is now relatively famous in his own country, he is little known elsewhere. In 1953, the late Kurt Wolff made a valiant and distinguished attempt to introduce Jouhandeau's writing to America, and failed. There were probably many reasons, but the most realistic is simply that Jouhandeau is caviar. As Claude Mauriac said in his *Introduction à Une Mystique de l'Enfer* (1938), "if a dozen contemporary writers escape oblivion, he will be among them. He will have innumerable readers, but at the rate of a few thousand per generation." Max Jacob once described Jouhandeau as "*un homme qui se devore,*" "a man who devours himself." He has published some sixty books, and though the earliest (1921) more or less observed the normal conventions of story-telling, the later ones have stripped themselves down to leanly *pensée*-like paragraphs which simply record and analyze the daily progress of Jouhandeau's household: there is Elise, his Xantippe-like wife, an ex-dancer dancer, fervent Catholic, and one of the most colorful personages in world literature; and there are friends, pets, an adopted daughter, relatives, as well as Jouhandeau's own urgent, if not very orthodox Catholicism, and his bi-sexuality. It amounts to a soap-opera, but an extraordinary one, ruthlessly annotated, making footprints in human psychology where literature has never walked before. A year or so before he died, Gide declared Jouhandeau his spiritual heir, though just what he meant, he did not make clear. At the least, though, Jouhandeau is an original, and the living French writer most likely to mean more and more to coming generations.

The less famous characters will explain themselves, and pertinacious readers may even want to look up qualifying accounts of some of the events in *other* people's diaries. Julien Green's *Journal* for 1951, Cocteau's *Journal d'un Inconnu*, Jouhandeau's *Carnets d'un Ecrivain*, among others, offer objections or expansions of Claude's record. Again, this may vex American readers. But if we are to know ourselves, we must not be pridefully coy about the sometimes ungainly apparatus of diary-keeping. Though it may seem narcissistic, it is also an extension of Socrates' tenet that the unexamined life is not worth leading. The French, of course, are undistressed, and as a matter of fact, one of the most delightful scenes in the book is the one in which Claude and his father are reading mint copies of Gide's *Journal*, just off the press, while Gide himself sits opposite them on the terrace, and presently all three go off to their respective rooms to—what else?—record their reactions.

What most amply, and finally, emerges, in any case, is a portrait of Gide in the flesh, and one which is worthy of, consonant with, the important role he played in our cultural life. We have already had important evaluations of his work and his character, but when, for instance, Sartre finds him "an irreplaceable example because he chose . . . *to become his truth*," we recognize Sartre's aspirations vis-à-vis his own writing, rather than Gide's; and when Jouhandeau tells us that "what he loved above all was a certain spontaneity of imprudence," we sense, not necessarily Gide's, but Jouhandeau's own subtlest instinct.

"*Comme le truite*," he once wrote, "*j'aime à remonter les courants*," "like the trout, I love to swim upstream, against the current." Claude Mauriac speculates, but he gives us a greater mystery as well: Gide as he looked, acted, dressed, spoke; Gide *pris au vif*; Gide, as it were, *a priori*, before any theory, or insight can simplify him; Gide flashing and glinting, in midstream, for each of us to net in his own way, for his own purposes, with his own need.

ROBERT PHELPS

xviii

PART ONE

Paris

Paris, Thursday / October 21, 1937

As my friend Jean Davray and I entered the Café du Rond-Point des Champs Elysées, he pointed out a man seated alone at a small table. "Look, André Gide," he whispered. I recognized him at once. There were two empty chairs separated from his table by nothing more than a passage for the waiter; we sat down.

I studied him with excitement. How often I had hoped I'd see him! There he was in front of me, showing his sensitivity to cold: that overcoat he hadn't removed, that woolly sweater under a maroon waistcoat— it came out the sleeves of his coat and half covered the backs of his hands . . .

I stood up. "Monsieur Gide?" He lowered his eyes. His face lost every trace of brightness. I felt that I had terrified a tortoise. From back in his shell an ashen face, expressionless, motionless, allowed an infuriated "Yesss?" to escape through clenched teeth.

"My father is your friend François Mauriac." My magic formula gave life to that wooden mask. "Excuse such a welcome . . . You realize that I must protect myself from . . ." He asked me how my father was. I feel

3

embarrassed and have only one wish: escape. But I don't want to say good-bye without introducing my friend Jean who's dying to be introduced. "Davray, was it? The one who wrote the book on Michelangelo? Of course. I know I wrote you a letter about it. I recommend it to everybody I see . . ." The ice is broken. From that moment we feel no reticence. Politics, our basically identical feelings on the subject, join us. Waiters and customers interrupt our conversation as they pass between our tables, but after each eclipse we continue.

"I always did have great respect for your father. But these past three months my admiration has increased. His articles in *Figaro* have a con-sid-er-able im-por-tance. Publishing them requires great cour-age, ex-tra-or-di-nary courage. That's a quality quite rare nowadays—we really have to tip our hats . . ."

I reply, alluding to Gide's break with the Communists after his return from the USSR: "My father will appreciate such praise coming from a man who has proven his courage in such a startling fashion. And what courage! How much the more deserving of praise since it made you run the risk of being accused of the worst a man can bear, betrayal! The Communist masses are sincere. They believed in you. Then, in the service of the truth as you see it, you did not hesitate to break with them."

The hand of Gide sketched a gesture of humility. He added, "You know, courage is nothing but a habit . . ."

Somehow I broached another subject, but after a word or two he confessed: "Don't say a word to your father. I've already been to two films this evening. I saw *Drôle de Drame*, then *La Dame de Malacca*. I've felt so lost, so alone . . ." Films provided an opportunity to

4

discuss the world at war. The newsreels from China
have affected Gide as they had Jean and me . . .

"I almost reached the point yesterday of asking your
father for his signature. But I feared I'd disturb him . . .
It's the business of *POUM* in Spain, the trial."

"*Parti Ouvrier d'Unification Marxiste?* I'm keeping
up with that . . . In *La Flèche* I saw the report of the
committee of enquiry sent there. Nin assassinated . . .
A mock trial arranged on the orders of the Russians . . ."

"You read *La Flèche?* That makes me very happy. It
serves the truth." It was saying that, that Gide looked at
me for the first time with affection. His eyes sparkled. In
the way in which he studies me there is something very
human that moves me. Obviously he's thinking "So, he's
on our side . . . Not the little Fascist I would have expected . . ."

"Why don't you write for it?"

"Bergery frightens me. After all, he is a politician.
And besides, one ought not commit oneself without
grave considerations . . ."

"But you have shown that you know how to disentangle yourself . . ."

"Yes. But one has to be careful about creating the
reputation of being a . . . a weathercock. But to get back
to the subject of the scandalous jailing of the members
of the *POUM*, I can tell you that Martin du Gard, Paul
Rivet, Georges Duhamel and I expect to send a telegram, asking only this, that the accused be promised a
trial. There will be nothing political in our request."

"I could, if you like, speak to my father about this, in
your name . . ."

5

"Of course I accept! His signature would add a great deal. It isn't too late . . ."

Suddenly he shows another face, his teeth clenched behind a strange tough smile, eyes glowing. "I prefer Hitler's methods. The assassination of Roehm was monstrous! But he did it openly. Hitler denied justice absolutely. He wasn't ashamed of the shameful law he used. On the other hand, there is nothing more revolting than the pretenses of the Stalinists. Those they bring to trial have all been condemned in advance. Laughable performances, masquerades . . ." He speaks of the USSR with extraordinary bitterness. "No advantages whatsoever will ever make me accept lies and crime."

I mentioned the disarming sincerity of André Chamson. Gide agrees, but adds that our friend Chamson's a bit naïve. But to my question whether the leaders of the Party in France are sincere, he shows some confusion. That is a question he has not yet cleared up. But there are others, the militant members who form the foundation of the Party . . .

"You can talk about 'sincere Communists.' They detest me! But what is the difference? In two years they too will change their minds. After my first book I was told" (by "my first book" Gide can't mean *André Walter*—it must be his first book on the USSR!) " 'In an hour Alessandri destroyed your arguments one by one. Not one piece of your exposé is left.' Well, not too long ago I saw Alessandri and he said to me, 'I admit I was mistaken. You were right.' Alessandri is now teaching at the Lycée Hoche. Since, as you say, you're often in Versailles; since you're a reader of *La Flèche* and thus have some comprehension of these things, visit Alessandri

6

and say I sent you. You will certainly profit from it. As a friend of Chamson it should be possible for you to bring them together. That ought to be interesting . . ."

I studied him one more time from my viewpoint of tongue-tied good fortune. That very morning I had been reading letters in which Jacques Rivière writes, "At a quarter to two Gide arrived accompanied, as always, by his exquisite simplicity . . ." And, suddenly, right in front of me: Gide, alive, *there*, exquisitely simple.

Friday / October 22, 1937

Once again I think of André Gide, of that hermit muffled up in negligence (which too has its chic), of his "I've felt so lost, so alone . . ." How tough old age must be for him. The isolation it produces at the heart of the greatest possible glory. A sadness like the sadness of that night: two different films, then a light supper . . . And around you a crowd that cannot know you, the blind world. It must be something like being dead already . . .

He said, "I used to subscribe to *Sept* and considered it a periodical of great importance. I learned recently with great joy that your father plans to revive it." And when I mentioned my friend Frédéric: "The first letter he wrote me was a masterpiece, both in style and thought. The second disappointed me . . . What he wanted was to establish a regular correspondence. There's no question of anything like that." On the other hand I could see that Frédéric must mean something to him when André

7

Gide pulled a sheaf of papers out of his pocket and handed me a page on which I recognized my friend's hand in violet ink only too readable, only too wise. Gide read the date, "September 18th . . . That's already some time ago and I'm carrying it around still. Please let him know . . ."

I had much less trouble obtaining my father's signature for Gide's telegram than I had expected. Since I had carefully followed the series of reports *La Flèche* received from the commission of enquiry sent to Spain to study the disappearance of Nin, it was easy for me to explain the business to him. Besides, Georges Duhamel had paved the way for me in talking to him.

I wrote Gide immediately, over my father's signature. I mailed the letter feeling happy to have been of some use in these circumstances . . .

Alluding to my conversation with Gide, my father said, "That's one of the miracles Paris offers which the Province never can, these chance encounters so pregnant with meaning and poetry . . ."

Saturday / October 23, 1937

At the café the other night, Gérard Bauër sat surrounded by friends and devoured us with his eyes, Gide and Davray and me. We greeted him with a nod, more than a little proud to be seen in the company of such a great man . . . Well, in *Figaro* this morning, his *Guermantes quotidien* evokes our evening on the Champs Elysées.

Rubbernecks are born, not made. There is a race of rubberneck artists whose works, inspired by nothing but life itself, retain like a gem life's active reflections. But there is another race of artists, these perhaps the more truly "reflective," who observe people and life once and are satisfied with this single occasion; and it is from the profundity of the consequences of their thought that they draw everything necessary for their art . . . Certain philosophers seem to have been able to get along without ever having made use of the rubberneck, and even a few novelists . . .

The other night, in a café, my good fortune placed M. André Gide before me. With lowered eyes that saw nothing he spoke to a disciple. Now I have always been a rubberneck, so I watched him for a long time and thought, as I did so, that he would have talked exactly the same alone in a cell, because it has always been his thoughts he followed rather than things. His drama takes place only inside. And when he finally does take a look at things, it's possible that he will be disappointed—as he has just been in Russia. Stendhal, who loved the variety of life itself, would never have been taken in in the first place.

My father is right: these encounters are rich in poetry.

Sunday / October 24, 1937

I telephoned Gide's to find out if my father's signature had arrived in time. When I heard that Gide had already left Paris I phoned Duhamel just in case my letter

9

hadn't reached Gide before his departure. First I had Mme. Duhamel at the other end of the wire, a bit surprised that I asked for her husband; then it was Georges Duhamel himself. He was happy to be able to join my father's name to those of Paul Rivet and André Gide. "Phone Magdeleine Paz. She's in charge of sending the telegram. Then be good enough to phone me again. I'd like to know where we stand."

Magdeleine Paz told me that the telegram had been sent three days ago. We arranged the wording of a further telegram, something to the effect, "With all my heart I agree with Gide, Martin du Gard, Rivet and Duhamel. Mauriac." The papers carried it under the following form:

> Five French intellectuals sent the following telegram to the Negrin-Prieto Government: "Demand immediately that the Spanish Government guarantee all political prisoners their rights to a fair trial and especially freedom and protection for the defense. With our sincere regards." André Gide, Georges Duhamel of the French Academy, Roger Martin du Gard, François Mauriac of the French Academy, Paul Rivet.

Wednesday / November 2, 1938

Received a beautiful letter from André Gide. I cannot resist copying it in its entirety.

My dear Claude Mauriac,

I stupidly misplaced your book before I finished reading it. I like to carry a book on my walks, but often that liking plays tricks on me. Into what hands could the book have fallen, with its dedication which enables anyone to return it, but also makes its resale possible! Horrors!

Be that as it may, since I'd already read more than three quarters with close attention, I am able to tell you of the deep resonance practically everything you formulate so well has found in me. To me your book seemed well thought out—and with feeling—then well written; in it you demonstrate a remarkable maturity of mind . . . and heart—a maturity I have found in those few articles of yours which I have read; in particular I think of your *Answer to Bernard Lecache* where the proportion, justice and level-headedness are surprising when one considers your years. I want you to know with what attention and affection I follow your career. I hope to see you again; no matter how pleasing the memory I retain of our meeting at the Rond-Point des Champs Elysées, I feel now that there was a great deal more we might have said and that we might have said it a great deal better.

André Gide.

Tuesday / November 8, 1938

Another letter from Gide replying to my immediate answer to the above:

Not at all! Thanks to our books there will never be a wall between us; and no shyness nor embarrassment either on my part or yours. I was just considering a re-union with Jouhandeau myself . . . But I would like to see you alone first and—will you be free Wednesday late in the afternoon? You can come ring my bell around 4:30. I will welcome you with emotion . . .

Wednesday / November 9, 1938

Rue Vaneau. André Gide came to fetch me in the little room where his secretary left me. Silent, icy, intimidating, he points out with a grand gesture the long corridor down which he walks behind me. "One more letter to sign. Forgive me . . ." And he's gone. On my own I take a look at the high-ceilinged room papered with books. The light is fading. The little bay window opens on a misty garden, gray roofs . . . Two minutes later Gide reappears, relaxed, jolly—he gives me his hand with affability. Immediately he speaks of Jouhandeau. Jouhandeau himself tells me that, after a long silence, Gide has gotten in touch with him. I cannot fail to see in this renewal of contact between the two men the working of my book. "He's invited me to dinner tomorrow night . . . You know his wife . . . Remember, I often saw her in the past, but never in her own house, you understand . . ." I explain to him that Jouhandeau likes to *show* Elise, like an exhibition. Gide rubs his hand over his smooth chin and says "That's just what I thought . . . Also, he let me know that he'd come by for me so that we could have a moment alone . . ."

I feel that Gide is intimidated by the thought of this encounter. He is afraid of silences, of the eyes of Elise. "You're a friend of the family, couldn't you get yourself invited?" I reply that it would be a great joy for me to be present at such a dinner but that it would be advisable for him to arrange my invitation. The situation must remain such that Jouhandeau, if he prefers, can refuse and enjoy the presence of no one extra at this reunion with a former friend. Gide agrees. "That has all the possibilities of being *very* amusing, an evening of just us three . . ." I watch him. His face rests on his hand; it is harsh, severe with a touch of tenderness, something childlike.

"Jouhandeau supplied you with the excuse for writing an interesting book. I'm happy for him: he doesn't have anything like the position he deserves . . ." He admits to being bowled over by the "In-des-cre-tion" of *Chroniques Maritales* which he finds less successful than Jouhandeau's previous books. "There are even some badly written passages—which should surprise anyone who knows his admirable French. The end is cut short. He has botched something extraordinary there, a magnificent novel . . ." Then he speaks in an amused sort of stupor of that astonishing household: "Theirs is a *singular* case which truly deserves to remain so . . ."

Then Gide brought up my article in *La Flèche* on the Jewish Question. He agrees absolutely. It seems Mme. Roger Martin du Gard is carried away by it. He asks me to send it posthaste to Jean Schlumberger, who is writing a similar article for the *Nouvelle Revue Française*. "His ideas may be very slightly but certainly profitably modified by reading it . . ." When I filled him in on

13

some of the unexpected repercussions caused by this decidedly philosemite essay, especially the furious letters it provoked, he told me in exactly the same tone of voice: "They are really frightening . . . As though the question could be solved by artificially quashing it!" He brought up old B.C. "with that appearance I needn't describe to you, that air of the dealer in carpets . . ." who holds that there is no difference between Jew and Gentile, not even externally.

On the subject of *La Flèche* he complains, and rightly, that Bergery published a letter of his without permission. My father has never forgiven Fernandez for doing the same thing. Gide lists other "blunders" of Bergery's; but allows him the defense of good intentions. No doubt however that he wants me to repeat everything that he has said . . . Everything wrapped up in courtesy. "Of no importance whatsoever . . . I wouldn't want to bother him . . ." A thought in appearance insignificant but at bottom quite sharp . . . and fleeting!

When I asked him what occupied him now he showed me the galleys of his *Journal,* which he has decided to publish—"although it is infinitely more discreet than Jouhandeau, all the same I'm rather daring and that bothers me when I think of those proper *éditions de la Pléiade.* Naturally I've cut a great deal. Certain portions of my emotional life in particular. But all the same what I left often goes too far . . ." I cross-questioned him in the hopes of discovering how he keeps his journal. "In a most irregular fashion—I only retreat to it during periods when I feel myself especially vulnerable. It has helped save my life; it really has performed the miracle of getting me afloat again. Thus, after the loss which you know I suffered since our first meeting on the Champs Elysées—" At the thought of his wife his face darkened. His cheeks sank, a sort of tragic pallor, tremulous . . .

"Yes, I was blotted out . . . Truly, I ceased to exist and I'm hardly reborn yet . . . And without that journal . . ." Then he sat down again and spoke of a false aspect his journal owes to never being written except in times of stress when he can't write anything else. Then this exchange:

A.G.: And you?

C.M.: I too keep a journal, but I write it every night and haven't missed one since the 1st of January, 1930.

A.G.: You do it the right way. But do you succeed in being sincere?

C.M.: To begin with I always was. Now I am a great deal less. It's a matter of instinct, self-preservation, an indispensable prudence. It's difficult to admit this to a man like yourself whose sincerity is so total . . .

A.G.: Oh! You know, I have the same difficulties. And then, something else happened to me: one day it occurred to me that my journal might be published . . . Since that day it changed—did so in spite of me. And besides, without knowing it each of us makes a choice among his ideas of the day. One carries over from one page to the next a continuity which certainly exists in our lives, but certainly in a state less pure. Thus there are epochs in my existence where my journal speaks only of religious questions, or again of the emotions, or again of social problems . . .

15

A fleeting allusion to his communist experience . . . "You're right," he told me "not to join Bergery's group even though they are the only group that's attractive— never join a party!" We speak of Marxism. I tell him what Alessandri told me: "This is a subject about which Gide possesses a great deal more erudition than is commonly supposed." Gide allows himself a humble smile. He appears to be flattered. He says, however, "I made a loyal effort. But I never was able to get any further than the sixth volume of *Das Kapital*." He speaks to me too of our meeting in the café—how many hypotheses in his troubled mind! "Were you really there by accident?" And about Jean Davray. Of my father he says, "I know perfectly well that he likes me . . . And besides he is the only person who understands certain things about me . . . So sad that our paths never cross anymore . . . Perhaps you will serve as a link between us?"

During the course of my visit the doorbell rang. The secretary had left so Gide sent me to the door. A young man hands me a card, he asks for two minutes of M. Gide's time. "I'll go see if he is in." At the end of the corridor, on pins and needles, Gide stretches his neck toward the angle of the wall—just a moment before he had told me, "I suffer from a terrible curiosity! It catches me every time . . . I turn away the tiresome . . . But I have to know all the same who's there!" He takes the card. He asks me, "Hugues Fouras . . . *Bouteille à la Mer* . . . Know him?" I reply that the magazine unites a few pleasant enough younger poets. (I remember that my father presided once at a dinner of theirs.) With this assurance Gide leaves me. I work out the dedication in the new book I've brought him. Almost immediately

Gide's there again: "He wanted me to preside at a dinner . . . Beyond my strength . . . Impossible."

The moment arrives when I feel I ought to go. I take my leave but before that, Gide, in my presence, telephones to ask Jouhandeau if he can bring me tomorrow night. Elise's scrunchy voice: "At whose request did you say?" With his teeth clenched he pronounces the word as only he is able, "At Monsieur Gi-de's." But Jouhandeau isn't there. Gide will call me if the response is in the affirmative.

There you are. It could have gone better. There were empty moments when our shyness blotted us out one as much as the other, and those contrasted so sharply with moments in which each of us had so many things to say. No letting go, no true confidence. But all the same the final impression is rather a good one . . .

At the very heart of silence, his comfortable study. I think of the cleavage which exists there too between the thought and the life. This socialist will die a bourgeois death. There is no longer a place in his existence for the unexpected. What a contrast with Jouhandeau! The other night while Elise and he gave themselves up before me to one of their regular household battles tailored to the measure of the visitor with a manner at once *grand-guignol* and tragic, it came to me what drama hangs over that house. *Anything* could happen to those two maniacs. She spoke of entering a convent. But I, I don't know why, imagined a perfect crime, or, at the very least, a violent death.

17

Thursday / November 10, 1938

When I arrived at the house in the Rue Commandant Marchand, Gide was already there leafing through a scrapbook in which Jouhandeau had pasted photos, letters and other mementos already faded and charged with emotion by the passage of time. Gide was seated; Jouhandeau stood beside him keeping an eye on his reactions. Did I make this up? In any case he seemed to me to discover on Gide's face—and in the occasional friendly words this or that item drew from him—an imperceptible irony. The preoccupied look on Jouhandeau's face was serious. There was nothing funny about it. Yet the old-maidish precision of his scrapbook, his excited commentary, all the methodical application to this pious industry distilled a sort of childishness which confused me, with Gide there—as though I were responsible for the greatness of Marcel Jouhandeau, as though nothing more than my say-so supported it and anyone could have told me, "You've deceived us! That man hasn't a spark of genius . . ." André Gide, fortunately, knows the books of his host and loves them. That thought reassures me . . .

Elise arrived, dressed up like the trained horse in a circus, frizzy-haired, painted. It was her best seductress outfit with peculiar golden clusters at the breasts. As soon as she saw him she informed Gide of how deeply his loss touched her—but she blared out her condolences with such jollity that our faces froze . . .

For dinner we had to go back downstairs. The meal

was served in a corner of their luxurious salon on the ground floor where furniture, bibelots, lampshades and cushions displayed the triumph of lyrical feeling. No food appeared without a long hesitation broken by the mysterious departures and arrivals of Elise or her husband. Long silences, pitiful conversation. I couldn't think of a thing to say and preferred to say nothing. Yet little by little the tone of our talk gained breadth and soon enough that extraordinary spectacle I'd hoped for began: the household brought into play all its charm and Gide all his attention.

With her calm cynicism Elise told of her mother and father—horrifying tales. For instance, how her mother was able to keep at bay a sadist who meant to rape her: "She let him get close, very close, then boom! she jabbed a pair of scissors into his body. He ran off bleeding. It was the same man who used to terrorize his wife, and no one in the village had the courage to interfere. During a particularly heated argument my mother decided she had the nerve to. She walked in: the poor creature stood there with flabby cheeks, in tatters. So my mother headed straight for the husband. She was carrying a pickaxe with which she dealt him a monstrous blow . . . In the end he killed his wife. He's in prison . . ." In this connection Elise mentions the sweating and frothing men who have tried to rape her too. "Not long ago," interrupts the man she refers to pompously as "my spouse," "she was out in the woods . . . now, now . . . And she saw a man . . ." Elise raises her eyes to heaven. For the twentieth time she proclaims her disgust for mankind, in deeply felt phrases like "Oh la la! I've had mankind up to here . . ." When she reached the scene

19

(which Jouhandeau has described in *Chroniques Maritales*) between herself and the father whom she hadn't seen for twenty years and whom she didn't even ask to take a seat, her speech took on epic proportions. "He had lost all he had, he hadn't a thing to his name: he was washed up but good. I told him so."

"You told him so?"

"Yes, I told him so. And I made him understand exactly what I meant, in spite of his whining . . ."

"After all, he is your father, isn't he?"

"My father, certainly, and I made it quite clear to him that he would never be forgiven by the daughter he abandoned. He went off . . ."

"And then?"

"And then nothing. That's all. He's never come back . . ."

Jouhandeau adds calmly, "Perhaps he's dead." "Perhaps . . ." says Elise. Her face sparkles with savage indifference.

All this time André Gide paid the closest attention. Sometimes he asked a short question, or repeated the end of one of Mme. Jouhandeau's sentences, or more often an astonished *"Oui,"* grave and mysterious, would escape through his clenched teeth. And sometimes too our glances crossed and a similar complicity united us for an instant: a little irony, a lot of amazement. For both of us there was the pleasure of being able to say that this time there was another witness there with whom one could compare astonishing notes. It would be impossible to claim that both of us had dreamt it all.

Jouhandeau followed his wife's monologue with excitement. In that face, chalky as an exhumed monk's, the tiny eyes burn like braziers. That man lives as he burns. He wastes away and for the time being it is admiration and who knows, even love, that feeds his flame. Never before had I so perfectly realized the ascendancy, the prestigious ascendancy that Elise has over her "Monsieur Godeau." No, the Devil is not alone in possession of his soul . . . However, she does go on. "One night—I must have been eleven—my father got home in the middle of the night. He came and woke us up, my sister and me. He said, 'I'm ordering champagne for everybody!' In a panic my mother shouted he was drunk. 'Me drunk?' And snatching up an oil lamp my father balanced it on his head. 'Look at me and tell me if I'm drunk . . .' Well," said Elise, "I looked at him all right and I don't remember ever having despised a man the way I despised him at that moment."

"I must have been thirteen when I told him, 'You've had one mistress after another, I know.' He answered with, 'What can you expect; your mother's hats are too awful.' He abandoned us, left for Russia. That's where he was when their Revolution broke out. His love was exotic birds. They were his joy, his happiness. He had a whole aviary full. During a house-to-house check a Bolshevik said to him, 'I want the whole world to be free,' and opened cages and windows. The birds dropped to the floor knocked dead by the cold before they could even spread their wings . . ." This fine symbol amused Gide and bowled Jouhandeau over. The indefatigable Elise got onto the subject of her tenants. She described the whole series and the grotesque and magnificent made me think once more, "No one has any acquaintance he doesn't thoroughly deserve."

Gide supplies another proof of this. It is now his turn to speak, and he speaks slowly, in a self-assertive voice that admits of no interruption. He emphasizes certain syllables. He swallows others. From between his clenched teeth his sentences escape as they can, hammered out, mutilated, peculiar, yet superbly articulated. So he too has had some encounters in this life which he alone would be able to appreciate. Witness this marvel which he relates—with the greatest simplicity: a shepherd in the Pyrenees covered a packet of notebooks with his scrawl. Astonishing journal, in which one sees life in the village and in the mountains, in which one sees a new religion created to personify the spirit of his flock . . . And the real marvel, of course, that this document should have fallen into the hands of André Gide: "What an extraordinary, what a magnificent study . . . One day one of his *lambs* fell into a crevasse and *died*. He felt an over*powering* surge of *erotic* passion that lasted as *long* as the cadaver was warm. As a result of that adventure he *possessed* every animal in the flock one after the other right down to the last old ram. An *astonishing* page relates his amours with a *trout*. This young man was haunted by the idea he might be *im*potent. There are some marvelous pages devoted to the subject. He *spied* on the village girls, he reported all their secrets with *love* . . . He even wrote verses, alexandrines, and not bad either . . . If I publish some selections from these notebooks (privately printed and as a medical case) I would explain what to my *mind* is interesting in a life like that: that a boy who grew up without any religious education whatsoever created his own religion—that's *exciting* . . ." Gide added that Montherlant was very interested in this story. Montherlant, who suggests that the *torero* and the bull . . . And who hasn't the least doubt that every shepherd . . . Gide complained that Montherlant wants to publish what Gide told him of this affair and in strictest confidence. Gide's reproving face, rather tense: plump chin, thin lips.

But how beautiful it became when we got to the Jews! At the time of this conversation every Jewish quarter in Germany was being pillaged with systematic fury. Ignoble vengeance that answered the murder, in Paris, of a German attaché by a Polish Jew. The image of synagogues in flames, broken store windows, and the thought of the gigantic sorrow of an entire people pursued us to the point that we hardly dared speak of it . . . But Elise accuses Léon Blum of being the cause of the deplorable state of the French economy and mankind in general. A sort of satisfaction dwells in her, "As for me, I love the poor . . . My table always has a place for the poor . . ." Jouhandeau's embarrassed, "Don't exaggerate, chère, you always exaggerate . . ." But she keeps it up in the same vein. Gide's face however grows darker and darker. Now he is even more tense than at the moment when he accused Montherlant. But he is beautiful, tragic, so tough, and showing a sort of amazement; perhaps it's sorrow . . . Jouhandeau feels that he's losing the friend he thought he had reclaimed. To the very end Gide remains on his guard. He doesn't give in again. In the meantime he attacks the antisemites. Those among them who are his friends cause him untold grief when they stir up such passions . . . Whatever may happen they are already responsible. Then follows a serious description, but touching, of the sorrows of this hunted people. Then, "Have you read our little Claude's article? *Our little* Claude has *written* a *re*markable article on this subject . . ." No, Jouhandeau hasn't read it. He never reads papers or magazines. Not even the ones in which he appears.

Elise throws in a word here and there. Nobody pays attention. And the face of André Gide in spite of a succession of gentle tics glows with a new excitement. He speaks of the nobility of this people, of the beauty of this chosen people, these elect. I devour him with my eyes and I love him. I love him for all the human understanding, for all the human sympathy right there in his face. Allusions to the social problem finish by lending his wooden face a new beauty. Elise all the same keeps up her contention that her house is open to the poor, that she has no reason to fear poverty, that mankind is corrupt. "You remind me," Gide says, "of the lady who reduced the social drama to a single sentence: 'If I have no more servants I'm not going to be able to knit sweaters for the poor . . .'"

We change the subject. Prophecies, magicians . . . Astonishing stories interrupt and connect. Gide spells out the curious coincidences which cause him to predict Hitler's assassination—for November 26th! Then he makes his good-byes. I accompany him. He puts on his classic hat with the broad brim, his cape. He tells me that when Elise talks politics she "distresses me profoundly." For the first time I'm aware of his great age. I feel he's exhausted. He admits his fatigue so I help him into a taxi.

Friday / December 9, 1938

Gide cordial from the first minute. Youth I'd never seen before in his step, in his face. I realize from the beginning that he is showing me his true simplicity. How much more of my sympathy this relaxed manner elicits than that watchful reserve which was all I had known until today. He says, "I have a question to ask you and it is made easier by the fact that at Cuverville my wife always served fish Fridays—because your answer will decide the choice of a restaurant . . ."

"I'll answer just as simply: it makes no difference to me whether I eat fish or meat. I would be lying if I told you anything else . . . And I admit this without the least pride—on the contrary. You can imagine that I saw in advance that this question might come up and I greet it as an occasion to discuss a problem more essential than many . . ."

We were in the staircase. He assures me that he knows a little restaurant near the Palais de Justice where we won't be disturbed. In the taxi I tell him my father would be happy if he would come to dinner with us. He looks satisfied to be invited but declines for the immediate future: "When I get back, of course, and with pleasure . . . But I've already departed—officially. And actually I will have in four or five days—after I've finished correcting the galleys of my *Journal* and put my signature to the house at Cuverville, a matter of inheritance. Then I'll cut loose . . . Where? All I know is 'far away.' Italy, Portugal, perhaps Morocco. Unreachable's the main thing. I'm so tired . . ." I reply that his youth just now had struck me. "Precisely," he explains and his voice is deep: he separates the words into syllables as if he wished to load a maximum of will power into each word. "Precisely. I feel excellent physically. I haven't felt so comfortable for a long time in this skin of mine. My state seems to be perfectly adapted to the work I need to do. But here in Paris each day is nibbled to nothing by stupid jobs. My precious time is used up in empty occupations, useless preoccupations. If you only knew what I feel I still have left to write, what I still have left to say! And time runs on: I'm more exasperated and tormented than I can tell you by the idea that these last moments of lucidity, of intellectual strength, of good health are being squandered like that! So I'm leaving to take advantage of whatever life I have left. Time runs on, time runs on . . ."

We arrange ourselves in the back room of the bistro. Through a large grille the kitchen is visible: the chef busies himself in an appetizing fog. We have the room to ourselves and the waiters who come to the grille for their orders. André Gide begins to remove his wraps. He takes off his scarf, his hat, his overcoat . . . Nothing exceptional . . . But then he takes off his waistcoat too, his vest. "I wish to de*liv*er myself from this *sweater*." And there he is covered with wool, *red* wool that gives him the appearance of a strange clown, more precisely of the famous Grock—whose watchful face suddenly joins that costume.

Since he discovers that he's forgotten his cigarettes he dresses all over again. I'm struck then that he feels the necessity of explaining that he'll come back, that our orders still hold, and that he's "leaving his sweater as a pledge." I come with him. He tells me of the interview he's given a Jewish paper in Geneva. He discussed there that article of mine in *La Flèche*.

No sooner had we left the tobacconist at the Pont Neuf than Gide realized he'd forgotten to pick up the matches after paying for them. More explanations which he feels called upon to give, in the style of a man afraid of being taken for a thief: "See, these are the very matches you gave me . . . I forgot to pick them up . . . Isn't that right?" What distrust he seems to believe surrounds him! Perhaps it is the result of years of being misunderstood and insulted. There is something about this man that calls to mind the hunted animal. People describe him to me as subject to avarice, but if that's so why does he always give two sous to round off a bill when only one would be necessary?

There we are back in the bistro. Simple but excellent meal composed of the *spécialités de la maison*: curiously wrapped chops which unwrapped reveal tender meat in a thin coating of mushrooms; cheese (he didn't have any), and *baba flambé au rhum* with cream. What simplicity, too, what reciprocal trustfulness in our conversation. I spoke to him about his *Journal*: "You have been very cruel to poor Jacques-Émile Blanche . . ." I think of the letter I've just had from him yesterday: he had tried to see me, I had proposed a day but that day his wife was seriously ill and no mention is made of arranging a meeting . . .

"Yes, you're right," Gide answers, "and I've felt some

remorse. I have nothing, positively nothing against Jacques Blanche—he has always been wonderful to me. He has attempted over and over to see me ever since we stopped seeing each other and I admit I've always discouraged him. About his painting—one cannot be cruel enough. As for his personality, on the other hand . . . And especially now I realize that the picture of him I offer is false because it is incomplete. In giving only that facet of his existence which touches me personally I have betrayed him. I'm beginning to wonder if I should not write a preface to the edition (*la Pléiade* is bringing it out in three months) in which I can explain this optical illusion, this deformity of journals. Notice that Blanche isn't the only victim. I had to cut everything that concerns my emotional life, more precisely those pages, so important, on my married life. By suppressing that essential aspect of my existence I've given a deplorably incomplete picture. At times I did myself violence: even on the chance of indiscretion I re-established a balance. Thus I restored that *awful* sentence, so serious that I had suppressed it when I brought out the journal in my *Oeuvres Complètes*. It was something that Agnès Copeau said to me one day: 'My husband asked me to pray for him—he'd might as well have asked me to write a symphony.' "

André Gide was silent, then began again with tremulous voice—pitiless, that voice—which sounded as though it welled from the deepest spring of his being. "No, I have no right to conceal words of such gravity! I will be indiscreet. So much the worse! Other things are more *important* . . ." Several times he repeated this *"important"*; I had the feeling that now I caught his very meaning itself, at its source as it sprang from his body and soul, before words have worked their betrayal.

He returned to J.-É. Blanche. Gide explained to me that any injustice he has done him comes from how wounded ("more than I can ever tell") he feels by Blanche's indifference to suffering and "poor people." Gide has an inimitable way of repeating what he said to Blanche: "But these are *poor people*. You don't seem to understand that there are *poor people!*" At that point we began an emotional conversation about social injustice. He said, "I understood as I read your articles that you have deep feelings on this subject . . ." And later: "You must have guessed that it was this anguish of which you have spoken which drove me to join the Party. What a sad surprise! One of the saddest of my life was discovering that precisely on this point the communists have no *real* solution . . ."

Then he spoke to me of Christianity, taking off from a remark some friend made: "What you asked of Marx, Christ alone could have offered you . . ." He told me of his admiration for the Church now that it was at last beginning to wake up to a mad world "so much so that the majority of criticisms which Gide himself had heaped upon her in the course of his career were no longer valid." He plunged into a curious discussion in which he attempted to prove that the notion of Truth is not essential to humanity in general, but that along with Justice it is a special attribute of persecuted souls, and especially of Jews and Protestants. He quotes passages from both the Old and New Testaments from which it is obvious that Religion never mentions Falsehood (it isn't a capital sin) and saves any denunciation for the moment when Falsehood harms another (false witness). Curious collocations of passages from Luke and Matthew . . .

And next we spoke of Faith, or rather I spoke of it, and he followed me with intense concentration, reserving his own thoughts on the subject, he informed me, for another time, since it was getting late and we had already finished dinner. I explained that I found no difficulty in the problem of which of the various sects was right. What could I care about heresies when the important point is simply that one believe in Christ and love him? If I have faith how can the theologians and their disputes touch me? I would bend myself to their commandments without hesitation, eat fish Fridays, and love would drown all useless questioning. My real difficulty, however, is in believing that Christianity is the truth. There is no doubt that my education has given me a longing for Christ. But desire cannot create its object.

Here and there Gide interjected a question. He did so with passion . . . His passion seemed excessive to have been excited by such banal sentences . . . They did not concern him; I did, inasmuch as I am a young man, and a young man representative of my generation . . . He whispered, "You are at the very heart of the problem . . ." Then we went back to his place. He asked me upstairs a minute to show me the cane that Francis Jammes gave him and which he mentioned in the last *NRF*. He mentioned that *l'Anti-Gide* of Francis Jammes (he had just died) signified his complete lack of comprehension. Hadn't he shown a complete lack of conscience when after finding no publisher for the book he asked Gide himself to place this indictment for him? Then to my father, for whom he feels deep gratitude for intervening in the affair of *l'Union pour la Vérité,* and Gide adds: "At a time when everyone heaped insults on me, he was one of the few to come to my defense . . ." And I told him very simply of the friendship that joins my father and me, then of the difficult position my father fills, of being "officially" a Catholic writer and feeling that to spare the pious he is taking a chance of betraying literature, of not dealing with subjects which obsess him, etc. How well Gide understands this. On the subject of Henri Ghéon he was even more exact: "He meant so much to me . . . How he has changed! I hardly recognize him. I haven't been able to follow him. Besides, he writes anything that comes into his head now. He never was one of those people with whom I could talk about just anything at all. We never did talk with each other about just anything at all." He told me Jacques Copeau was "an awful man." And Claudel? He still admires him as a poet but detests him as a man: "I have a whole drawer full of letters from Claudel. We never see each other." He tells me how Claudel one evening in front of Paul Jammes, his godson, set the brandy aflame on a crepe at dessert, saying, "This is how God will handle André Gide!" After that Paul Jammes wrote Gide his first letter (they hadn't met, Gide had just joined the Party): "I've made up my mind that those people are dreadful; I can love the ones on your side . . ."

Last of all Gide asked me to attend a lecture by Jules Romains tomorrow night. He will be there. He says "Au revoir" with such artless affection, so resonant . . .

This evening marks an end to all comedies of shyness and distrust . . . Yet probably not an end to the comedy which each of us puts on for the other: I do because his presence is glamorous, he does because he is old and my youth revivifies him. The affection which I feel for him loses nothing thereby in depth or sincerity. As for him . . . I'd have to know him better (or not know him at all) to decide . . .

Saturday / December 10, 1938

By accident I got to the theater where the lecture is scheduled, the Pigalle, at exactly the same time that Gide got there. I gave him a copy of Francis Jammes' *Morceaux Choisis*—it's extremely rare—for his *Anthologie*. The line is very long and I don't have a ticket so Gide offers me the fourth seat in his box. He introduces me to his party: Mme. Théo Van Rysselberghe, and a rather clumsy young woman who looks too much like Gide to be anyone but his daughter—the same young woman my father mentioned having seen with him the other night at the dress rehearsal of *Testament du Père Leleu* . . .

In the foyer with Gide smoking a cigarette. "Bonjour" for Benjamin Crémieux. Many people come over to repeat "Maître" to my friend. He acknowledges each greeting with exaggerated friendliness and holds out his hand at the wrong moment. Resolved to recognize everyone he even recognizes some who don't recognize him. He talks to me about the letters of Jef Last. The galleys have just reached him and he finds the translation so bad that it must be begun again from scratch. Just as we get back into his box for the second half of the lecture he asks me, "Aren't you embarrassed to be seen with me?"

Jules Romains walks out and comes face to face with the mahogany theater, which resembles a piece of expensive furniture. His voice sounds thin . . . Easily made criticisms of postwar politics. Gide had said, "This could be very exciting—the title of the lecture indicates that Romains is going to tell us exactly where he stands. No doubt about it, he's going to come out as a Fascist." But Jules Romains refuses him that pleasure. The talk drags on without the speaker allowing himself a single opinion that is either original or personal. Just as a certain Pierre Dominique whose book I was reading a day or so ago, he advises France to renounce her interests in Eastern Europe and turn toward her Empire. The solutions which he proposed were falsely bold, politely revolutionary and deeply conservative. He played on words. He shied at no facile phrase that he felt would wring a laugh from an audience stupid enough to accept his flatteries with pleasure. His poverty of invention astonished Gide. First he showed great attention, his chin in his hand, his index finger forcing a deep furrow up his left cheek, then he made a face and repeated "Oui . . . Oui . . ." with long muffled vowels, then he turned to me and whispered, "What a clever man! He has discovered a method for avoiding every real problem. He runs away from every position where a clear answer is expected . . ." And shortly thereafter he got bored: "I am desolate: to have dragged you to this . . ."

The lecture ended late. I had to make hasty good-byes. I'm afraid that I got away a bit clumsily . . .

Saturday / December 31, 1938

Letter from André Gide. Among other things he writes:

I'm drawing up my balance sheet for 1938. As you know, it was a year which brought me great losses. Against so dark a background the joys stand out all the more; among them, rare as they are, not the least has been your friendliness; I want you to know that. I have been kept in Paris, by business first, and then by the flu which has not yet given up its hold on me. Twelve days of bed and of a dullness so total that I could not take up a pen to write you. As soon as I was able I left the Rue Vaneau and took a hotel room in the interests of more peace and quiet and there I am still, keeping to my room as a precaution . . . I feel still, and for some time to come, that I am "out of this world" but not so far out that I could forget you . . .

Thursday / March 9, 1939

Postcard from Luxor: "I will not be able to return to Paris until after the Easter vacation. Distantly but un-forgettingly, André Gide." That gidian *"unforget-tingly"* delights me.

34

Thursday / April 27, 1939

Phone call. I tell Gide I'd written him two days ago when I heard he was back: "I was expecting a letter from you . . ." His warm voice, so touching. Agreed to meet at his apartment tomorrow morning.

Friday / April 28, 1939

I waited a minute in the morning room. The harsh voice of André Gide hammering out a letter came to me from the next room where he dictates.

He walks in as soon as that's over, dressed in a suit of frieze that has something about it of pajamas. A bright red foulard at the throat. The jacket was a color half between that of the scarf and the maroon of the trousers.

I stayed an hour. Mutual embarrassment prevented any relaxation from one end of our conversation to the other. He discussed his refugees with me (he is concerned with the futures of numerous exiled nationals) and I listened, but this conversation merely filled in the silences. Once I did take a bolder tack:

c.m.: The past year brought me the happiness of making your acquaintance . . .

a.g.: Yes, we were made for each other's understanding. I found that out at that delightful dinner—you remember . . .

35

C.M.: I do remember. But we see each other so infrequently, hence this diffidence . . .

A.G.: You needn't rub it in! Moreover, I fight against myself to force myself to seem more at ease than I am by nature. My shyness saddens me so: I ought to be telling you so many things, some of them very intimate. We understand each other well enough for mutual confidences . . . And we waste our time on thin remarks . . .

Then he turned his head slightly—which indicates his charming modesty. I said, "We mustn't try to go too fast. We have time. Who urges us to? A single visit cannot use up all our friendship . . ."

I mentioned his promise then, a dinner at home with us. His face brightened. That proposal seemed to gladden him; it touched him, especially when I added that as I had said before he would find no other guest, only Mother, my father, my sisters and Jean . . .

"Your father . . . Yes, I'm sorry we don't see each other more often . . . But between your father and me there is—no, it's all on my side—a sort of *appréhension.*" Only Gide can use the word *appréhension* in this unusual way, thanks to his pronunciation. "I'm always afraid of seeing him again, for fear that we won't have anything to say to each other, and that would be embarrassing, or on the contrary that I would say far too much right off, that I would entrust myself too intimately, that I would confess things far too serious."

Then he came to the announcement the new Pope made concerning Spain. I tell him how my father and many other Catholics were grieved as much as any of us. How was it possible for the Vicar of Christ to glorify Franco without the least reservation! The Pope spoke of the crimes of the losers as though there hadn't been atrocities on both sides, as though—and this would be the least he might have done—there hadn't been a single Christian on the Republican side where in reality there were many who in good faith upheld their legitimate government. As for me, I had read the Pope's letter with anger but without real sorrow since "the pope" means nothing to me. My father told me, "I understand very well that the Holy Father would be constrained to be diplomatic. But a single word in the right place, perhaps a sentence, and so many hearts straining for justice would have found peace. In place of this: nothing. Nothing but inexcusable betrayal." Then he took the line that he must give up suffering over this and how deceptive this new stance is! "So much the worse!" he says. "This too we will renounce . . . The Church has always been like this. How could we have counted on anything else? This cannot touch our faith. In the case of Spain we cannot expect infallibility, can we?" But this simulated indifference cannot hide a wound that still aches. Again last night my father said to me, "I used to be surprised at the unanimity of praise reserved for Pius XI. Now I understand the grounds for that world-wide admiration. Yes, he was a great Pope who returned to the Church her former glory. While Pius XII, who had my confidence . . ."

André Gide reveals a similar distress. His face is marked with suffering: "How much evil his attitude will cause! I've come to regret the good I said of the Church in the last pages of the volume of my *Journal* that's about to appear. Yes, I was wrong to make amends . . ."

Later: "This journal? A huge block of me . . . The tone's rather whiny and that scares me. I never kept it that I wasn't desperate." I asked him about another *Journal,* Julien Green's. He complains of the subtitle under which *Figaro* printed an excerpt: "André Gide, slave-trader." "I fully realize that it's meant ironically. But readers very often read no further than a title. It *could* do me an injustice. Very distressing . . . Besides, Green seems to have failed to understand all I meant. All I did was attempt to bring to his attention that the Negro workers were often so badly off that as slaves they would have been better treated . . ."

In an about-face easily understood by someone who like myself loves deliberation, qualifications and above all justice, he speaks with frenzy of an article in *Révolution Prolétarienne* in which a Negro accused French doctors of mutilating, robbing and generally persecuting the Negroes: "Such generalizations are not to be borne," Gide says. "Let him name names, let him document with cases. Amen. But I won't have him include every doctor in the colonies in his accusations! I know some of those doctors and they're heroes . . . I would like to reply to his article but I don't dare. They would just publish my letter under the heading 'Andre Gide, slave-trader.' . . . Humph! Really, Green has done me a very dirty turn . . . Now I don't hold it against him but it does cause me pain . . ."

Gide is always afraid that he's going to be condemned for the wrong crime.

Then he read me a letter from Roger Martin du Gard, who has settled in the French West Indies. Climate, solitude, a new life demanding that one get used to it, all described. The breathtaking news that arrives from Europe in the laconic Havas dispatches evoked. Martin du Gard writes that these reports, shorn of any literary value and of all details, sound as absolute as the summary before each lesson in the history book. Each paper gives him the same unhappy surprise, but only for a short time, because it is of the nature of surprise to be brief. This is to be preferred to the obsession he felt throughout the end of his stay in France and so on . . . For a second Gide hesitates. He smiles, then he decides to read on, with irony, a bit embarrassed, politely shy: "There he says that the natives are charming and that I would have some incredible temptations . . ."

We talked about Cocteau also. Gide's face brightens with real affection: "What a charming creature! I like him, I like him in spite of everything . . . I am unable to hold anything against a magician like that, not for long." He tells me though that he never was able to take either man or work completely seriously. That is the sentence I hear most often passed on Jean Cocteau.

How many things are contained in an hour, and in an hour during which "Shyness prevented us from speaking!" I've left out thousands of interesting details. For instance, to remark on his humility—"humility" never reached his lips in a situation in which Cocteau wouldn't have avoided the word: cleverer to suggest—which prevents his ever believing that an action of his can have real results, whence his amazement each time his intervention on their behalf saves an exile he values from being expelled from France. This time it was a

German translator whom he shared with Giono until Giono signed a contract with a German publisher whom this translator considers "Nazi"—he's that "pure."

At the end of my visit renewed confidence flooded his features. Overcome once by his shyness (is he joking?) he attempts to thrust aside the temptation to make confidences, escapes from one fragmentary avowal, returns, picks up the words again. Then, suddenly bolder, he admits, "I wrote while I was in Egypt and Greece . . . How shall I say . . . It's what our friend Jouhandeau would call *Chroniques Maritales* . . . But in a different key entirely . . . Unfortunately they're not publishable . . . Some other time, if you're deserving—but you are already . . . Yes, I am going to read it to you!" With a malicious chuckle he then showed me a manuscript "young Schwob"—he means René Schwob!—has entrusted to him. "He believes that it's 'scarcely publishable'; he's shown such bravery in admitting the inadmissible! We'll see . . . I'm always skeptical. I'll be very much surprised if he really goes very far . . . They all say that. And then . . ." He makes a gesture with his whole arm, worldly-wise, ironic . . . The author of *Si le Grain ne meurt* has the right to talk like this.

He confessed to me that he believes he's finally going to have to give up the journal form, and when I look incredulous he adds, "True, I did keep my *Journal* every day I was on that trip . . ." Concerning his travels he adds that loneliness spoiled them. "Alone in Egypt I was unable to make use of the experience. I need someone to talk to. Otherwise nothing has beauty or even interest. It wasn't like that when I was your age and went everywhere alone . . ." In Greece he had the company of a young Greek, teacher in one of the islands: "We spent several days together at Olympia . . . That was wonderful."

We recalled that Greece which I too love so much, then I said good-bye. "We haven't managed to say anything yet," he whispered, "but we have re-established contact. *A très bientôt.*"

As the door closed behind me I noticed that I had been there one hour *exactly*.

Tuesday / May 2, 1939

Gide calls a meeting off: "Called to Perpignan in the interests of one of my refugees." I admire greatly the devotion of a man as spontaneously egocentric as he is.

Tuesday / May 9, 1939

How can I begin to describe that family dinner Gide graced? He rid himself quickly of shyness and acted at ease in our midst. I'd never seen him that young, jolly and relaxed. We got onto no elevated topics and it was well: stories of pets of his busied us at dinner. During the evening he told us particularly of his love of movies. He never misses a new one. He knows every film and the names of actors whose names don't appear in the credits. He recalls also his own memories of the theater, racy ones, "because my contacts with the stage have always been sorrr-owowow-ful . . ."

Politics and religion hardly entered our conversation: Gide merely alludes to the disappointment Pius XII caused him; he surprised my father with the name of a new Catholic leftist publication, *Le Voltigeur*; he declares that he will invite me in the near future to dine with the principal private secretary for the Ministry of the Interior, M. André Dubois, who ought to be helpful in the enquiry *La Flèche* has commissioned from me on the conditions of foreign nationals in France . . .

"Men like that, men who have such a place," my father said as soon as Gide left, "are hunted. They're expected to behave in a manner worthy of their reputations. On the other hand, they're always glad to be able to escape from these obligations. It was obvious that Gide enjoyed himself tonight making mere conversation. I recall the look of a beast pursued he had at Pontigny when Du Bos brought him to bay and demanded they settle out of hand problems of the most serious nature, life and death . . ."

My father added: "What strikes me most in Gide is his incredible youthfulness. He's seventy now, think of it! And see how fresh he is still, like an adolescent . . . The childlike side of his personality moved me again tonight. How charming he is! It makes me sad to think that 'good people' won't receive him. They say that 'his books dishonor him.' But make the comparison between him and 'good people': imagine the twisted features, close, deceitful, wary, frightening features of Chaumeix; M. Gide at least has been honest. He has been what he is . . . How much *greater* the *bad* people often are than our little saints . . ."

Gide kept sliding off the divan where he was seated. He chain-smoked his oriental cigarettes. Then with a twist of his back he straightens up. I catch sight of that healthy young face of his with its lower lip which juts out. His mouth is extraordinary in that irony; contentment, or happiness can change it so swiftly. In his presence my father became a little boy; he no longer sought to shine; he spoke of his accomplishments with an unwonted humility. Gide listens badly or not at all, or rather he doesn't appear to be listening. Grunts of approval break into his silences. He recalls with a naïve refinement the disappointments, weak points and deceptions of his *métier*. He talks money with a simulated avarice. I terrify him when I mention that the restaurant where he intends inviting me with M. Dubois would be prohibitively expensive—in a private dining room!

"How's that? Les Capucines? Gallimard himself recommended it, it's a ressssstaur-rant I never heard of."

"You don't know Les Capucines?"

"Nnnno . . . Gallimard tells me it's next door to the Paaaaramount."

"Eh bien, cher Monsieur . . ."

"All right, it is possible at 50 francs a person and in a private room at that . . ."

"What do you mean 50 francs! Three times that, sir, three times that!"

"That won't do; it simply won't do; it's too expensive . . . It is against my principles to spend money like that in a ressssstaur-rant . . ."

43

I can't imagine why I've included this piece of dialogue: it's value depends entirely on the inimitable quirks of gidian pronunciation. And then for that avarice that is too much part of his myth to be authentic. We never took it seriously. The truth of the matter is that Gide makes fun of himself no less than we make fun of him. But on this point he meant to be taken seriously: the innocent really did believe that in 1939 it was still possible to lunch in a private room, at Les Capucines, for 50 francs.

One of Gide's traits that continues to strike me is his fear of boredom. It feeds his love of movies. It has gotten to the point where he speaks greedily of committees and lectures which he hurries to because they supply "a very real diversion." When I praise the cabaret of Agnès Capri, he is immediately intrigued: "Mention it a-gain, when the time comes . . ." Add to all this that other feature of his personality, his curiosity and there he is—almost.

He left at 11:30, looking quite happy with this evening. Mother and my sisters found him agreeable. My father rediscovered a forgotten charm.

Wednesday / May 10, 1939

Gide has made a conquest of the entire family: Claire and Luce never tire of mentioning his charm and Jean says, "That was a *historic* evening."

Taken down as well as I remember: the story of his

trip to Perpignan. Every train was being run in two sections because of the Eucharistic Congress in Algiers. He made the trip down in a compartment stuffed with priests and elderly churchgoers: "It was then that I realized that my trip to Perpignan too was 'pious works' . . ." He hadn't gone on behalf of a single refugee, there were several, and he was unable to locate any of them besides, since their camp had been transferred to Bayonne: "Thus the whole journey was in vain. That ought to teach me to be enthusiastic! There are decidedly moments when I feel I must be an enthusiast . . . My good fortune embarrasses me. I hate myself for having nothing to do. It is then that I shake myself and say 'Up you go, go and try to aid those who suffer!' That is the reason I left Paris the other day." He told this without any affectation whatsoever, and with just a touch of irony.

When I told him that Garbo made me cry in *La Dame aux Camélias* he exclaimed, "Me too! Naturally . . . But that happens to me so often in the movies. And I'm rather ashamed of my tears, afterwards, when the lights go on . . ."

Tuesday / May 23, 1939

When I got back to Paris there was a letter from Gide waiting for me, written curiously enough on the back of a souvenir postcard from the restaurant Calvet: He's given me an appointment, Rue Vaneau at 7:30. My first impression on seeing him again was one of emptiness, of

45

having nothing to say, and besides I was preoccupied without meaning to be by my examination tomorrow morning. Nervous about disappointing him, especially when he said, "Before my trip to Egypt and Greece it was clear to me from our conversation that we could agree about the great issues . . . Then we didn't see each other again, and next we barely saw each other at all . . . This evening too there will be a third party . . . But I do hope that today's meeting represents our entrance into a new phase, will be a preparation for our seeing each other again very soon."

We stayed at his apartment a few minutes. He took me up to the studio Marc Allegret used to live in. A trapeze still hangs from the ceiling—I felt the need of some physical fitness . . . Gide explains that having Marc this close became impossible when all those film people began to use his own library for a waiting room.

We talked about Martin du Gard, whose address is simply General Delivery, Fort-de-France. I tell Gide that Martin du Gard's absence was an unpleasant surprise touched with sadness for me, that I was always encouraged by the knowledge that a man of his importance, grand as he is, followed our exertions. Now that he's left France I'm almost indifferent to writing for *La Flèche*. André Gide doesn't even listen, he follows his own thoughts and regrets. "His departure left me completely at sea," he says. "I had gotten used to the idea that some day or other I would escape to his place at Bellême and stay on there forever . . . And suddenly he's gone and I'm alone . . . What a help he was at certain periods of my life! He was able to advise me, aided me; I could always confide in him . . ."

Outside. Gide speaks of his *Journal* that's about to be published: "I'm very much afraid . . . I expect the worst, even that I'll receive challenges from a great many seconds at the same time!" I'm not sure he was joking. More exactly, I feel that the knowledge I have of his suspicious nature points enough in the direction of seriousness. No, there was irony in his remarks . . . "What *you* made me add were a few lines on J.-É. Blanche, lines that improve the picture . . ."

We talk about Simenon, then Giono, but I'll pass over the interesting exchange we had at their expense. I must get to essentials. A slow walk up the Boulevard Saint Germain had brought us to Calvet. M. Dubois wasn't there yet: Gide led me out and sat down beside me on the first bench we came to. I was touched.

I was touched because just a moment before, in fact, just as we crossed the Rue des Saints Pères, Gide's voice became conspiratorial and close to the heart. What he confided was something he had already said, during our last encounter. Had he forgotten? I don't believe so although he did use almost exactly the same words this evening: "I'm going to show you something . . . Very serious subject . . . What our friend Jouhandeau would call *Chroniques Maritales* . . . In a completely different key, of course . . . The other side of the coin . . . I would like to know what you think. I was under a compulsion to write it all . . . For a long time the thought of a final elaboration has obsessed me. And now it's done."

He spoke slowly, a pause between every sentence, stoppage caused by so much between the lines, every word more precious for all that.

Now on the bench under the eyes of unfeeling passersby and a beautiful summer night he goes further in his trust. His eyes turned aside, he speaks. He tells me how grateful he is for me. He tells me I mean very much to him. And I don't understand, I really don't understand a thing, except that no gift could have startled me more than his astonishing friendship.

And then suddenly an unexpected question hits me: "Claude, did you know that I have a daughter?"

"No, certainly not!" That spontaneous lie alone saved more insupportable embarrassment.

"Yet your father knows . . . He's never mentioned it?"

"No."

"All the same, I know he knows . . . I'm aware that at the première of *Père Leleu* at the Comédie Française he did notice the young lady with me. I'm certain that he was struck by our astonishing resemblance, her *outrageous* resemblance to me . . ."

I kept to my lie. No, I knew nothing about it. My father's sense of discretion prevented him saying a word about it. How this fact amazes me, etc. . . . . "May I ask him about this?"

"Please do. A moment ago you brought up how exactly my thought matches your father's, how that astonished you the other night. You cannot guess, I'm sure, nor can your father, how much deeper this correspondence goes. I want so to speak to him about it . . . We will have so much to say to each other . . ."

After what was probably an allusion to the development of his religious ideas (but I could be mistaken) he began to speak of "la petite Catherine," his daughter, "whom you will of course meet in the near future."

Could he really have forgotten that she sat in the same box with us at Jules Romains' lecture! And when with a feigned inspiration I blurted out, "But wasn't that young lady . . ." he gave in. All these lies embarrass me. I'm not sure what I ought to say. Then I added stupidly, "Yes, I recall . . . She did seem attractive, lost in thought, intelligent . . ."

André Gide pretended he hadn't heard the obtuseness of my remark nor its clumsiness. He said, "Yes, she's a curious child, I'm sure." Then immediately after that he said, "But how she has suffered because of me . . ." Remember, we are sitting on a bench all this time, across or almost across from Calvet. Down the boulevard the church of Saint Germain raised the beloved shape of its massive belfry against the pallor of the sky—and I wished for a flight of swifts to round off a beautiful day. However, there was Gide, penetrating deeper and deeper into self-revelations . . . I held my breath, said nothing, held still for fear of startling him.

"When I think that Michel Arland wrote 'André Gide, with all his talent, will always lack an understanding of what it means to suffer.' When I think that he dared write that, *believe* that." Despair on Gide's face, sad and tender face, when he said that. "My little Catherine caused me horrible sufferings. I lived in terror that my wife would find out, you know, that she knew I had a daughter . . . *Hélas!* I was never able to ascertain whether she had suspicions—perhaps she knew for certain. The drama between us took place in silence . . ." Will I ever be able to forget the muffled tone, a bit too calm, saying, "Silence made the drama we played out between us"?

49

Then he made an uncertain gesture, got up to tear himself from his revery. "Let's go. M. Dubois ought to be there by now. We aren't going to be able to say anything else tonight. We really must see each other again very soon, all right?"

But he was mistaken: M. Dubois was running behind schedule. M. Dubois wasn't there. In the private dining room on the second floor, among the light-hearted murals suggestive of amorous rendez-vous, Gide continued his revelations. I will never forget the picture: Gide, his head hanging, uproots word after word in spite of his teeth remaining clenched in a last-minute effort to keep them back. Nor will I forget the mechanical gesture with which he accompanied these words: his knife played back and forth in the folds of his napkin as though he meant to cut them like the pages of a book. And what did he say next? He said (and his words were momentarily disappointing since his concentration had led me to expect even more serious revelations), "No one has seen the journal I'm going to show you—no, I have read it to two friends . . . Jean Schlumberger especially . . . Precisely in cases like this Roger Martin du Gard was of great service with his advice . . . I'm not sure whether it is possible to publish a piece like this . . ."

Again I kept to myself my surprise in realizing him so concerned about publication. A man of his stature should concern himself with the truth of whatever witness he bears, without a care to whether his message reaches print or not. I am forgetting the part which the unnatural plays in a writer's make-up, and also something which Guéhenno points out in his most recent book: a particularly gidian trait which makes him do all his thinking out loud—that explains Gide as well as discovering something unnatural about him, and I prefer it because it's more elegant. But Gide goes on . . .

"What bothers me most of all—what bothers me is that in regard to this drama my wife and I played out I make revelations about myself and the development of my existence that terrify me. I give up awful secrets . . . I give them up in spite of myself . . ."

I no longer felt the least disappointment. I understand what causes Gide's embarrassment, what keeps him fiddling with his knife in the napkin . . .

A.-L. Dubois, assistant secretary to the Minister of the Interior, Albert Sarraut, interrupts our scene. He is a bright-looking young man with a musical provençal accent. I had expected the worst: but here was a man. A man liberally endowed with heart and soul. He is in a position where he can accomplish much that is good—and he does so. Gide had already told me of the time André Dubois had spent preventing the imprisonment or expulsion of many of the refugees Gide had taken a particular interest in. "I have been wanting to do something for him. So I invited him to dinner tonight . . . After much hesitation I must admit. I'm always doubtful of my importance . . . My astonishment was considerable when I saw his joy and haste in accepting . . ."

Gide shows him telegrams and letters from refugees. Dubois who has already worked overtime at the Ministry graciously allowed this extension of his daily business—certainly he would enjoy talking with Gide about something other than his own official affairs. He promises one phone call here and another elsewhere, to do all the leg work, and Gide loses himself in gratitude.

He wasn't very sparkling, Gide wasn't. He had just mentioned his insomnia to me, and told me about his migraines. He was burnt out. Dubois was interesting: we discussed the laws relating to aliens. He puts at my disposal his entire documentation in the Ministry of the Interior for my article in *La Flèche* and the doctoral dissertation I plan. When he returns from Corsica he will give me a ring: he leaves tomorrow for ten days. Before he leaves he'll send me that valuable collection *le Code Pratique des étrangers.* His kindness shone in every act, his conversation fascinated. On the conditions in Spain now that Franco has won he was able to supply news available nowhere else. On the Munich crisis of last September, he supplied this pathetic insight: Daladier at the telephone waiting for dispatches in anguish, as unprepared, as ignorant of their exact significance, authenticity and meaning as any reader of *Paris-Soir!* "There are times when the decision *Peace or War* is no longer within human power . . ."

Gide doesn't show signs of life until Dubois admits to having been much amused by *le Treizième Arbre,* a little play that was given recently, and which Gide himself had advised me to miss. Indeed, hadn't he been the very first to walk out? He looks delighted: "Oh yes . . . That's what everyone says . . . They all do laugh . . . All told it was almost a success!" He laughs through his clenched teeth.

We walked on a while through the night. Gide left us at La Place Chappe. He disappeared at an exhausted pace in his shepherd's greatcoat. Dubois and I sang his praises. One thing I said, perhaps rather naïvely, was "The miracle is that he has no idea *who he is*. His excessive humility is astonishing. We are used to the haughty bearing of lowly pen-pushers. And lo and behold the greatest of living writers, André Gide, is self-effacing, well-behaved as a beginner."

Dubois agreed and went on to describe his own surprise and embarrassment the first time Gide appeared in his office a few days ago: "The idea that I was actually seeing André Gide overpowered me. He meant so much to me all the while I was growing up. I was moved, very moved at making his acquaintance, but all I saw before me was a man who begged my pardon for wasting my time, a man who asked for what I would have proudly done, and done a hundredfold, as though it were a singular request. He acted self-conscious and that and his air of humility increased my own nervousness—I probably behaved as if I were feebleminded."

Friday / May 26, 1939

Gide called. I had written him yesterday to thank him for dinner. How solemn his telephone voice is—it's so correct it makes me nervous. It says, "Will I be able to see you toward the end of the day . . ." No, unfortunately. And tomorrow I leave for Vémars. But tomorrow morning would be fine. "Good . . . Tomorrow morning then, if you say so, Rue Vaneau, any time after 10:30 . . ." His haste to see me again surprises me. No

53

matter how good an actor he may be, our relationship has passed the stage of mere coquetry. Really, could a real friendship develop, one not based on the fact that I'm young and the ephemeral advantages of youth?

Roger Lannes takes me to Versailles where we're expected for the evening by Jean Cocteau, who had fled there to work in peace. We arrive about 6:30 at the Hotel Vatel, where he has a room. The little staircase forks, splits again in two, changes its mind from floor to floor as it leads us through an intricate maze right to the open door that framed Cocteau in profile against a background of smoke. A blue cloud floods his shuttered room and suffocates us with a new odor, mysterious and even a little sweet. The close atmosphere drove the beauty of that ending day out of our minds. Cocteau says, "I just smoked my sixtieth cigarette . . ." He opens a window on an empty street worthy of the most distant province. The night allows a bit of its purity entrance.

Impeccable gray trousers—half unbuttoned. A belt unbuckled hanging out here and there. In shirtsleeves with a small blue sweater—it fits too snugly. His untidiness is as astonishing as the disorder of his hair. Cocteau starts talking. He will continue until 1:00 A.M. without letting anyone else get a word in edgewise, with the same dash, the same overflowing spirits. The euphoria which follows work well done lends even more humorous eloquence than usual to his conversation—and that's already saying a great deal. But the Cocteau style remains ever the same, copious and dependent upon memory, as always in an orator of genius. Sometimes he will speak extemporaneously without knowing what he is going to say and it will come out as though he were reciting a part from memory. He knows that part very well, so well that he can allow himself some extraordinary ad libs. While following in the main one of his established "conversations," he will make additions much in the manner of an ancient poet embellishing a myth every time he tells it.

On the dresser among detective stories and cheap editions of Racine and Molière the manuscript of his new *Potomak* fans its great white edges. On a table five or six of those drawing books I remember from my childhood, gray covers decorated with an eighteenth-century *montgolfière* rising in print: that's the manuscript of his new play, *La Machine à Ecrire*, which he just finished without an erasure in five days of unceasing work! "The magic framework the Parc de Versailles supplies made that miracle possible," he admits. "The clockwork, the devices of this astonishing creation give themselves away alley by alley. The statues are caught forever in their unchanging amusements. Their clever remarks have been turned to marble once and for all and Versailles as a piece, transcending the years of its tenants, lives with a life of its own—like a ship without crew pursuing its useless course through time . . . I went for a walk and when I got back my play was born of itself. It unfolded according to the same precise necessity. Who ever will define the importance to an artist of his surroundings? It was only chance that brought me back to Piquey recently. None of the other beaches on the Bassin d'Arcachon had room for me. So there I stayed and now I know why: the new *Potomak* was trying to catch my attention. Where else could I have written of Radiguet better than in the very room where we spent the summer? So I stayed on in Piquey in spite of the cold and lack of comforts right up to the moment I put the last period to my new book."

The new *Potomak*—suddenly he takes it into his head to read it to us! The speed of his delivery, the obscurities of a work in which every sentence contains a private allusion to a real person or event, all that confused me. From time to time I could grasp a single splendid sentence as it flew past, one of those weapons with which poetry strikes us hard, right through the heart. Or I smile because he has told us whom he intends by the Vicomtesse Méduse. Carried away by his work he runs right through ends of chapters. This outpouring of images, these fireworks Cocteau disguises with his voice; his voice is thin, clipped, precise, inhuman; occasionally a child's laugh breaks this monotone: Jean Cocteau isn't unhappy with his new book and he doesn't mind showing it. "God knows I loathe Voltaire," he exclaims, "and nothing could be further from my thought than his skepticism. But I have tried to recapture his tempo, that *speed* in which he was past master. This new *Potomak* throws off sparks like a blaze of dry twigs—and that's exactly what I wanted."

Jean Marais walked in halfway through this reading. We all adjourned to the dining room where he ate hurriedly—he must be in Paris by nine for his part in *Les Parents Terribles*. Cocteau, Marais, Lannes and myself, taken all together make quite a stir in that well-mannered dining room with its mirrored walls, its chandeliers and a décor recalling country hotels of the Second Empire. Little old ladies wearing religious-looking outfits, doubtless readers of *La Croix*, a whole world of pensioned bourgeois ate their dinners in a silence like death. Our party welled up into this slumber with the shamelessness and racket of lunacy. In particular it's Cocteau's woolly head of hair, his brazen voice, the aggressive handsomeness of Jean Marais, and the wasted features of young Lannes that cause the stir. The more timorous probably believe we are demons sent as ambassadors by Hell itself. The mirrors reproduce our faces around us—and suddenly my heart sinks as I realize that young man whose back and neck are so unfamiliar *is me.*

"Jeannot" has to leave for the theater. We had been waiting a long time for Pierre Guérin, a fellow I don't know, who had accepted an invitation for dinner. Tired of waiting we decided to order—it was nine by then.

Reproducing Cocteau's conversation is too much to hope for: it flows, or rather it overflows without let-up, always with that same delivery which heaps up telling images, paradoxes—and lies. The truth automatically becomes false simply in passing through that conjurer. Does he know he's lying? I don't believe it. Lying is inherent in his nature. He tells a lie as poetically and beautifully as a merle sings. I believe that one proof of his good faith is the way in which he never tries to keep his stories even *possible.* For example, when he exclaims, "And that's why I live here in Versailles!" after he had described the literary life in Paris in the caustic tone of an ascetic, he can hardly expect us to have forgotten that he is in Versailles to write a play and that as soon as the play is finished he will not lose any time getting back to Paris. I believe he believes his own stories. He is an actor, but he plays with real sincerity.

I can only set down the most important points in his endless monologue. Those that touch André Gide, for instance. In that quarter I can no longer believe in the perfect innocence of our friend Cocteau. There is an ill will perfectly obvious in his tone of voice although he tries to mask it with protestations of friendship for Gide and even turns it into a good-natured childlike humor. The reasons for this ill will do not seem unselfish. I felt there was jealousy there—and my heart hardened for an instant, I felt such shame and inexpressible anguish.

In the meantime Cocteau had accused Gide of jealousy! Cocteau pretends without the least sarcasm that the success *Les Parents Terribles* has scored is keeping Gide awake nights and that Gide cannot place the play *he* wrote although he takes it from director to director. He reproaches Gide with having written an *Oedipe* right after his own Oedipus and cannot forgive him even though he quotes Gide's humorous reply, "What can I say, my friend, it's an—oedipémie!" Cocteau is certain that the success of Marcel Proust and the important place Proust has in the NRF list distress Gide, that he threw a tantrum when it was decided that there should be a statue of Proust in the publishing house while he, Gide, is only honored with a bust! He adds that it was Gide who politicked for the candidacy of Paul Valéry at the Academy in the secret hope that he would not be elected, and when he was Gide took it badly. He revenged himself with a remark: "Dear friend, you have played a round of The Winner Loses . . ." And that isn't the half of it! He claims for instance that Gide has always managed to run with the hare and hunt with the hounds: that during his, Cocteau's, battle with the surrealists Gide played both sides in an unfriendly manner, that Gide's exchange of open letters with him after the war lacked dignity, that Gide was lacking enough in candor to attribute a recent date to a letter which he, Cocteau, had written at seventeen, and this in the *NRF* and that this change of date changed everything, and that Gide defends the Encyclopédistes united against Rousseau, joining ranks (and with reason!) with Grimm and Diderot, and confusing (with some grounds . . .) Cocteau and Jean-Jacques. Once on this subject he claims that Gide was sent on a very long journey by the *Nouvelle Revue* just to dissuade him, Cocteau, from publishing his rehabilitation of Rousseau. Cocteau refuses to believe that Jean-Jacques suffered from paranoia; no, he really was persecuted! Gide refused to allow himself to be convinced and even maintained, as though he'd been an eyewitness, that Rousseau died in an ignoble fashion—Cocteau used a very crude expression which I'd rather not write . . . All that recited with appropriate imitations of Gide's vocal explosions, all that mixed as well with praises of Gide's *grandeur, génie* and *haute dignité* and then, without transition, incredible anecdotes carefully chosen—or made up—to demonstrate the shabbier sides of this great person!

I can't write it all! I will have to pass over the astonishing tales concerning the Daudet family except to quote Mme. Daudet as she "made a little room" by burning a folio of water colors, "worthless things that poor old Cézanne gave Alphonse to pay off a debt"; about Barrès, except that Cocteau considers him an extraordinary man "who sold his soul to the Devil," and except this thrilling confession of Valéry's: *"Monsieur Teste?* The beginning of a novel I couldn't finish . . ."* but there was so much more.

Pierre Guérin arrived as we finished dinner, so we had to sit while he ordered and ate his. Then we went back upstairs: one little light suddenly gave back his youth to Cocteau along with its gentle shadow. His hardened mask, twisted and dressed up in the embarrassing ruins of a false childhood, of a youth destroyed from within which has left nothing more than an empty shell—this gave way to a face almost beautiful and in any event *young.* His slender frame, and everything lithe and frisky in his make-up abetted this illusion. I remembered what Marie-Laure told me about Cocteau's former good looks.

Mirrors, filled with mystery by this half light, filling the room with a mysterious fluid, were they a fountain of youth—no, it was the water of eternity . . . Meanwhile, of course, Cocteau went on talking. If you will only add a barked *"Quoi?"* at the end of almost every phrase; thrown in, I suppose, to allow him to breathe (it comes out mechanically) ; if you will scatter a handful of "Don't you see's?" into his lectures and, rarer, a *"Mon chéri,"* which astonishes because he means *you* and you are not his *chéri,* but this is pure absentmindedness on Cocteau's part, you'll have something like the following: "After the *maîtres* we have inevitably the *petits-maîtres:* monks aped by monkeys. The masters have genius, the same genius childhood possesses: Gide, now isn't he the old English lady who travels in a hat with a green veil to see the pyramids? Claudel? Isn't he really Baby Cadum?* And Valéry's just a distracted schoolboy who raises his hand to leave the room. The true masters are *invisible.* That makes sense: nobody wants the fashions to change, everybody is used to the status quo. Today Rimbaud is *visible,* and it's my turn to be invisible. Do you know what the doctors mean by a 'flesh wound'? The bullet that's clean and fast enough will pass through part of the body without leaving a trace: the flesh closes of itself. That's an image of my work: invisible, it's so clean and so fast. And that's to be expected. Ah! Rimbaud is not easily gotten off our backs! Look at the young poets of the moment . . . Rimbaud is a chewing gum that sticks to all feet, and it won't come unstuck. But what he has meant to us! What other bondages he has delivered us from . . . Thanks to him we meet images head-on without recourse to 'like' and that's great. But the surrealists by their excesses ruined it all. Radiguet came and saved me from them. Without Radiguet I would have gone on looking for combinations more and more baroque, to writing three-word poems on postage stamps . . . At the time that we met Radiguet no one was writing simple stories or simple poems. As soon as he came a way was opened in the direction of purity. At last I understood that every mystery, all poetry, every miracle of the ineffable could be expressed, or better: suggested, without any contortions of the mind or the heart. Without Raymond Radiguet I never would have reached perfection. '*L'Ange Heurtebise,*' for instance, is a very beautiful *object,* a poem

* The fat, smiling baby of a contemporary advertisement. *Trans. note.*

without a blot. It is so pure, so beautiful that any thief who came with the intention of imitating it would simply circle it and never find a flaw through which he could get in. Not to be imitated, a miracle like that simply isn't to be imitated! *'L'Ange Heurtebise'* is suspended between heaven and earth like a tremendous crystal-mint lifesaver at the end of an invisible string . . . But people are unable to *see* a thing like that. I'm *invisible* . . . And all the same it's monstrous! Now Giraudoux doesn't know a thing about the Supernatural and writes of fairies without ever having met one. Giraudoux is a poet for capitalists, he's a ten-cent store for poetry. And of Giraudoux they write (and they're serious and he allows it): Giraudoux writes with blood! But as for me, I'm always 'that amiable clown.' Me, Jean Cocteau, who have given myself body and soul to my work. Me, Jean Cocteau, who never hesitated to challenge Death itself to a duel! And I sit here waiting for the worst Death has to offer after writing the last pages of my new *Potomak* where I take on Death on its own terms, where I actually invoke Death—what I had to say was so pressing. And I am a bit worried, but it's for Jeannot's sake. But as for me, Jean Cocteau, what's the difference? The only value as far as I'm concerned is dedication to my message and *basta*! That's why I loathe a Voltaire or a Goethe so . . . Nothing could be further from me! Gide once said of Goethe that perhaps someday it would be proven that Goethe was only a tin horn big as the column in the Place Vendôme. And people laugh at my exertions! It's never *my* blood that they discover, just Giraudoux's, and his impossible *Ondine* receives unanimous praise . . . I wrote to Jouvet about it. I said what's the use of lighting up that stupid palace from the inside when no light comes through his characters—they have all the transparency and life of stones . . . But me, I'm a jester, oh yes. Marvelous! One day I asked Colette how it was she hadn't written anything you could exactly call a masterpiece in spite of her tremendous talent—she took me to a mirror and said, 'Look at yourself. Now me, I want to enjoy life, to have beautiful legs and a healthy body. Now look at yourself. You haven't even kept anything comfortable to sit on!' She understood that I've become a mere pen from my devotion to writing and that my very blood has turned to ink. And Giraudoux, considered the ascetic of poetry, is not even *real*! It's marvelous . . . Giraudoux who doesn't even know what automatic writing is! Now without that you never have a masterpiece, not a real one with a voice that carries. Do you really believe that everything in *La Princesse de Clèves* or *Adolphe* was *planned*? What boredom, what sorrow, what coldness! But the unspeakable grace of these works which have every sign of being cold, sad, and boring proves that something divine has been at work, this mystery that not even the author himself fathoms and which makes him say more than he intends. That's how it is with my *Machine à Ecrire*. That's how it is with my new *Potomak*. That's how it's been with everything I write . . ."

Meanwhile he walks back and forth; or instead, he stretches out on the chaise longue while the laws of perspective give importance to the soles of his shoes that ought to result from hallucination—and recalls drawings in his *Opium*. He talks and talks, his eyes lost in the smoke, his features on fire. He laughs, he grinds his

63

teeth. He makes fun of himself. He mimics. There were three of us there as spectators but he addressed us in the singular! In his eyes we were "the public" and he addresses his public with the familiar singular . . .

I am leaving out innumerable mentions of the book I am writing about him. He groans with the injustice of life: to think that Gide and Valéry are the subjects of books while as yet he, Jean Cocteau, has never been seriously considered by a critic. He suggests a very simple explanation: while the work of Gide makes many concessions to the demands of the moment and never goes very far into the unknown, his own . . . That famous *acte gratuit,* or so they call it, which made the fortunes of *Caves du Vatican* makes him laugh: a real gratuitous act would have been pushing a young man out that window, a radiantly beautiful young man, not that old bag of bones! Tossing that old bag of bones off the train was no *acte gratuit,* it was a simple hygienic reaction . . . I will not detail his unbelievable anecdotes of Picasso and Stravinsky (whom he accuses of cheating at the moment he resumed work on *Le Sacre*—or did he say began the orchestration? That he resigned the glories of the Invisible in order to be seen and produced a minuet instead of the grand and savage music of creation) nor any more of Max Jacob than the picture of him trying to lose a child whom the Stravinskys had adopted and then quickly tired of: the child believed they were playing hide-and-seek. He would pop up laughing and then disappear shouting "Coocoo!" Then for a while he followed Max at a distance. Jacob thought he'd shaken the child at last when suddenly he had the wits frightened out of him by an unexpected little face.

That's all in the new *Potomak.* Cocteau read us this passage at the end of our visit. Propping himself against the wall he bent over the bed where his manuscript had found a place: the back lighting gave his features the cleanness of a shadow-box figure. His profile cut its well-defined crests against the light. At this point Jean Cocteau reminded me of a little child, a sickly little child.

Marais walked in, back from the theater. *Les Parents Terribles* was over. I was dead tired. Guérin took me back to Paris in his tiny car. Lannes could have stayed on: he never grows tired of this act which he must know by heart. As for me I've had more than enough. Again the lack of authenticity strikes me although a reading of his works had dispelled it. In which phase am I a dupe? The other night at *La Revue de Rip* a loathsome comic gave an imitation of Jean Cocteau. It is easy to imagine the shame of such a caricature. Tonight there was one thing though which redeemed many of my doubts and many of my questionings: the face of Jean Cocteau. His true face molded by sorrow or joy, his *human* face. That face at least we must take seriously.

Saturday / May 27, 1939

André Gide receives me in the morning room that pre-cedes the office of his secretary. And for the first time he seemed to me at ease from the first. He spoke simply and

65

without doing violence to himself. My frozen features made me ashamed and a discouraging shyness angered me all the more for being new to me. But Gide seemed to notice none of this.

A table stood between us. I felt like I was taking an examination. Gide signed a letter, then he began to speak of refugees—their situation concerns him. He entrusts me with a letter from one of them which I am to relay to André Dubois whom I'll see again before Gide can. Other letters litter the table and they all have a common origin. "I will never again have the leisure to accomplish anything else. My time is eaten into. But what right can I have to turn my eyes from such suffering?" He reads at some length a letter concerning the pointless despotism of the police—I'm to take it to Dubois. "Don't fret . . . We are going to talk about other things . . . Come: my study will be a more congenial locale . . ."

I precede him down the long hall. "Sit down over there . . ." He points to the most comfortable chair and sits down in front of me but a bit to the side. I feel that the situation is at last more confidential. He talks about "his little Catherine": "She hasn't read a thing I've written—except *Symphonie Pastorale* . . . She asked me for a copy the other day after seeing the film the Japanese made from it. But she never said a thing to me about it: I have no idea what she thinks. But she *is* very intelligent . . . I've given her free rein in choosing her reading. But she is only fifteen and I often can't help saying, 'You should not read that book . . . You will get much more out of it when you're older . . . All you're doing is spoiling a masterpiece . . .' Until recently she was unhappy to ever discover anything of me in her. For instance the time she saw that we signed our names alike even to the flourish and period. Now very recently, on the other hand . . ."

All that is not lacking in interest but both of us know it isn't what we're there for. It's my turn to talk. I attempt a comparison of Catherine with my sisters. We're just beating around the bush. I take a look at him: he's wearing a black velvet waistcoat and has covered his shoulders with a thick blue shawl. He looks embarrassed. I'm not giving him much help. But little by little the ice breaks again and we feel free to be open.

"Your letter moved me deeply, Claude. I want you to know me better, to see me as I am and not just through my writings . . ."

"But I have learned to recognize you in your books: and I have found you as I knew I would. You came as no surprise . . . I was already fond of you. I have learned only—to be a little more fond of you . . ."

"Be that as it may. I find myself at ease with you and it almost surprises me . . . You are so much closer to me than for instance your father can be . . . To him too I hope I shall be able to talk . . . But before that I know I will have to undergo veritable labors of approach. Whereas you and I—why, we're going like a house-a-fire."

"It may just be possible that I understand you, could understand you completely . . ."

"Your letter was yet another proof of that."

"To get back to my father—he's very fond of you too, you know . . ."

"I do know. The shyness between us results from my age—and perhaps from his too . . . I can only feel close to young people. But that he and I are very dear to one another I do not doubt: at the end of one of our visits to Pontigny during which we had both remained on our guards I came up to him just before we broke up and said, without meaning to, and simply because our silence had been too much for me, 'I like you so much, Mauriac . . .' And he answers 'And you mean altogether too much to me . . .' "

There was a silence, then he said, "I don't want to let that manuscript I mentioned out of the house . . . But if you have the time . . ." In three minutes there was an empty chair before me in which lay the blue shawl. Off the cover of a little notebook I read a careful handwriting that's so well known: I was struck already by that style I recognized as unique. A dull silence hung over the room, the apartment and the whole city. Gide praised the nobility, the grandeur of his wife, Madeleine. He described the love he bore her, the essential character of which was its total divorce from the flesh. He expressed his remorse: since he sought, and found, his pleasures elsewhere, he was happy, but it never occurred to him that his wife could have need of anything more than this platonic passion. He never even imagined, at this period, that she was like any other woman . . .

A short time before his marriage, however, he felt the necessity of confiding his fears to a doctor. He confessed the direction of his amorous interests. He asked the doctor whether such a nature was compatible with the married state. He was told that his scruples were fantastic, that as soon as he was married he'd never think of such things again. Grave mistake in diagnosis: the psychiatrist's theory has not conformed to the facts . . .

André Gide described next his complete impotence faced with his wife. He does not go into details but one guesses that he had, so to speak, no "carnal knowledge" of her. Madeleine suffered but never thought of blaming anyone but herself, at first. "I am not attractive enough . . . It's all my fault . . ." Still ignorant of the true nature of her husband she was able to tell him after reading *Nourritures Terrestres* that this was one book of his which didn't catch him at all . . .

Gide came back shortly on the pretext of picking up his shawl. "No, no, it's not coquetry—I'm really chilled to the bone!" Then he was gone. But at that point in my reading he came back and sat down in the study, a short distance away, on my left. I could feel his presence as he turned the pages of a magazine: his heavy breathing punctuated the silence. I didn't dare look at him—I was embarrassed.

I was embarrassed because the story had become very personal: I wondered where he could have found the strength to sit there beside me while I made myself master of the saddest periods of his life. Not that I ever wanted to chuckle, nor show offense, nor pass judgment: my admiration remained as *total* as my respect. If I felt pity it was not for his life that I felt it, it was for the sorrow that accompanied it.

He tells of how their wedding trip saw the triumph of his true nature. I can't remember which of the Italian towns it was but he spent some time in the square where painters choose models. The one he picked was asked to come up to his room and be photographed. His poor wife spent day after day alone . . .

From Italy they moved on to Africa. One day in a train two schoolboys played in the next compartment, half naked in their open shirts. By leaning out the door Gide could touch them both: his caresses moved from one shoulder to the next, that was the worst he could do, but he found it so overpowering that his expression must have been frightening. In their hotel room that night his wife told him that he had had the appearance of a maniac or a murderer—those words cut deep.

There follows the rehearsal of that *drame du silence* he mentioned to me the other night. It spread out over their entire life. His wife never asked him a question. She stopped reading his books in order to ensure his complete liberty. As for him, he combined that disembodied love (yet more concentrated than passion) with the pursuit of his pleasures, elsewhere and according to the laws of his nature.

Madeleine lost herself more and more in the love of God, and more and more lost touch with her husband. The picture he gives is that of a woman different in every way from the woman he loves and from his own ideas. The judgments she passes are beyond appeal. Sure of the truth, she is uncompromisingly strict. Wounded by any departure from traditional behavior. In a word, "conventional," but worthy as most women are in that environment—which I know so well. Actually she was very limited in her charity while Gide, because of love, did not see her that way. He has complaints against himself: he loves her as she is. At last something opens his eyes and he realizes his cruelty. Her love for him is perfectly natural, she would have liked to have borne his child. She had been forced to transfer her unused maternal love to a nephew. But there is one thing that Gide does not confess in a confession which goes as far as this does: the child which he refused his wife he gave to another. That supplies the climax of the drama: the story rises to the level of an ancient tragedy. Just before he put the manuscript into my hands Gide said, "This is a very strange story, a story whose meaning transcends its actors . . ."

I read. Gide fidgets, coughs, sighs in this silence. I read the end of this drama which stretches over decades . . . Gide attempts to draw closer to his wife as she draws further and further away into piety. She gives up taking care of her appearance. She sacrifices herself. She never listens to what her husband says: his advice, his pleading, break against her, or rather slide off her impenetrable indifference. She never says no but she does consider his wishes null and void. Gide is desperate to see the delicate hands of his wife performing the coarsest tasks and gradually losing their shape. Tired of the struggle he finally gives up . . .

Only a short time before her death they approached one another more closely, or rather she approached him. The insults heaped upon him on the publication of his book on the USSR made a ground of understanding. But the *silence* continued. Never a mention, much less explanations: but Madeleine allowed him to dress the poor varicosities of her legs and her twisted body, Madeleine showed with her looks that she was grateful. And

71

this happiness was enough. He loves her more than ever. He loves this disfigured old woman as intensely as he loved that young girl who no longer exists. He wonders how love continues to flower in the absence of what appeared to be its cause, physical beauty. He wonders if it weren't simply her soul he loved all along . . .

Then she died . . . Here my own thoughts overlap the story: I have no idea any longer what Gide has written; all I know is that in one sweep of the eyes I have his whole existence, an existence to which the final period has been placed now that his wife, who had been the center of his life since adolescence, is no longer here. I have seen him in his truest solitude. I whispered, "To think that Marcel Arland . . ."

He sighed. He says, "Claude, I'm happy. Now you know me better. You will come back and read the *Journal* which follows, the passages I had to remove from the volume that's about to appear; they round off what you just raced through . . ."

He wanted to know if it were possible for someone like myself who knew nothing about all this beforehand to understand the development of this drama. I told him that all was clear, every word pregnant with significance . . . And I added, "I'm sorry not to be able to say more . . . I am far too moved . . ."

Actually I had the feeling that I had disappointed him, that I had not shown myself worthy of the trust he had in me. And then, as I left, we had this short exchange:

C.M.: Obviously, on our human plane all has come full circle; it's over, all over . . .

A.G.: Yes, all over . . .

C.M.: But there's still the metaphysical level . . . It could all begin again there . . .

A.G.: There's that level still, true . . .

He cut me short and pushed me out the door. Later than you think . . . I had to take a taxi.

Vémars, Monday of Pentecost / May 29, 1939

In *Si le Grain ne meurt* I read these lines which are even more touching after what I learned on Saturday: "In this little being [who was to be his wife but they were now no more than children] whom I already cherished, I felt the presence of a huge and intolerable anguish, a sense of disappointment which it would require every bit of my love and every moment of my life to cure her of . . . Until that day I had wandered in search of adventure. Suddenly I uncovered the reason, goal and devotion of my life." He adds that there is to be found the secret of his destiny.

Letter to Gide:

I am sending you this note by Mother who returns to Paris before me. I'm afraid it won't tell you a thing about what Saturday meant to me because I do not know how to express myself about what I read: you seemed to penetrate so deeply into each of your torments, to unravel their meanings so perfectly, that my talking about them isn't any use. I would have liked my looks and the few words I stammered to have made you understand this.

73

Now as to the lucidity of your testimony: I must tell you that because no words are ever more lucid than yours precisely, because you go to the very limits of your being in confession, the one silence you do maintain, the existence of the little Catherine, falsifies your story. It is impossible to gauge its tragedy, and its grandeur, without knowing this fact. But I am not unaware of what serious considerations prevent you from completing this account. I only want to point out, or rather show you, that it did not escape my notice—showing you once more how inevitably any attempt at sincerity runs into a self-generated obstacle. But perhaps you have put this matter into the parts of your *Journal* which I have not yet read or perhaps there were hints which I overlooked. I was so deeply moved—and your presence so near disturbed me so—that I might very well have missed the most important point . . .

Monsieur, my father and I the other day shared a lovely dream that concerns you . . . At the end of June we leave for Malagar. Malagar means terraces of vines rising before the most beautiful view in France! Malagar means fine days full of work, everyone on his own until the relaxation meals provide, meals that are tasty but never heavy because we all need clear heads for our work; and these further relaxations: walks along the stream at the end of day, the most touching sunsets I know, then beneath a sky the most full of starry holes I ever saw . . . Now this is the dream my father and I each had without any coaching from the other: That you should share this visit with us. We each told the other what this would mean to him. It would be wonderful. Whether this remains a mere dream depends on you alone. *A bientôt. I remain your most respectful and affectionate friend.*

Paris, Wednesday / May 31, 1939

From eleven in the morning to three in the afternoon with Gide. A single sentence of his can sum up the sense of this interview: "Usually the young people come to confide in me, and that's to be expected. But it isn't at all natural that I should be the one confiding in a young man of your age. But all the same, that's the way it is: you listen to me and I do the explaining and explain myself intimately, very intimately . . ."

The moment I opened the door I caught sight of my letter, exhibit A, on a table. After beating a little around the bush Gide came to the point. He took up first of all my objection to what I'd read the other day. He has nothing to say when I reply: "You have told me that you wish to publish this story in order to put an end, for good, to all misinterpretations either well-intentioned or propagandistic which have grown up around your relations with Mme. Gide. You have said 'The truth, the whole truth—is always better than any lie. This finishing touch is necessary.' Now then, I've pointed out that you haven't told the whole truth, that it has been impossible for you to do so for very easily understood reasons. So what good was this half confession?"

He mumbled that I was right, that there always is a point beyond which confessions never venture. He added that he was not happy with these pages, that they falsified the truth they did contain and to show me what he meant he showed me a letter from Madeleine, a touching letter she wrote him in 1918, the crisis year of their drama: "My portion has had its beauty," she wrote. "I have enjoyed the best of your soul, the tenderness of your childhood, and of your adolescence. And I know, that alive or dead, I will enjoy the soul of your old age . . ."

Then Gide tells me of his self-doubt, of the difficulties he now experiences in writing. He began to speak under his breath when he mentions the play which has occupied him for so long: all the social concerns with which he loaded it at the time he began writing now weigh it down and he tries to set it moving again by cutting; but that's painful work. "Mme. Théo Van Rysselberghe— our little Catherine's grandmother—a lady whose opinion means a great deal to me, read the rewritten portion of the play just the other day. Her reaction was a blow: 'I advise you to discontinue work on this . . .' That's what she said."

He sighs. His voice loses more volume, but another emotion makes it vibrate *con sordino:* "Claude, some days I ask myself do I really have anything left to say, haven't I brought my work to completion? A verse of scripture obsesses me, where the rest that follows the vintage is spoken of. After the vintage . . . I chew these words over all the time . . . For three years now I've been unable to write a thing that pleased me. The book that turned into *Geneviève* was to have been long, a very long novel. I burned it all. It was bad, very bad, awfully bad! I've destroyed a great deal else, a great deal else . . . You suggested a continuation of *Si le Grain ne meurt* in which you believe my marriage could be contained and not betrayed, and you added that this could be done without sacrificing either details or interpretation, both of which you consider necessary. That would be work too complicated, too delicate. Roger Martin du Gard in the extraordinary journal he's keeping has done the job for me, I believe, when he noted down all my conversations on this subject—this involved and mysterious subject! There were three days in particular, in the country, when I stayed with him; I told him everything, in detail, about this unbelievable situation . . . Claude, I have my doubts, I do have my doubts . . . And I must tell you how much your presence means to me and your affection. Both of them may help me, help me so much . . ."

At that point we reached the exchange with which I began: the extravagance of the situation in which the roles of confessor and confessed are reversed. Then he said, "At Malagar, if you read my play—and I will read it to you, I'm certain; the atmosphere there will, I hope, be favorable for a resumption of work on the play—it is important that both of you, father and son, have the courage true friends must have, and tell me if necessary just as cruelly as Mme. Van Rysselberghe just what you think of the play."

You see we had spoken of Malagar already. What emotion Gide showed (shamefaced but still overflowing, that joy) as he accepted the idea of a visit! I found Malagar for him in the pages of an old atlas. Again I sketched in the pleasures of a life of work there—with its reward, evenings of good conversation. "I'm allowing myself to be persuaded, I *am* persuaded! You know what a poor piece of wreckage I am: why should I refuse?" He asked me for details, dates, and then we told each other (just as my father and I did a few days before) what the stay there would mean for each of us.

As for me, I could hardly think about it without emotion and a lively curiosity.

But he also told me about this play, "this difficult thing I'll never bring to completion." When I mentioned the rapidity with which Cocteau writes Gide didn't hesitate to say that's how it ought to be, in fact that he himself had written his best play, *Saül,* or most of it, in a single day. Gide thought a moment and in a whisper he made this surprising confession: "I have known what jealousy means . . . for Michel. You might say he was my creation. He meant a great deal to me. He was only eighteen then. Then he met Cocteau. And to seduce Michel he deployed every grace in his satanic power. You cannot imagine how seductive he was when he was younger! Soon I felt Michel straying from me. He had always admired Cocteau, and the glamour with which he surrounded the name had the effect of casting me as a ridiculous old long-hair among the dead ancients. How can I tell you what I suffered! It was terrible. Jealousy is terrible. I believe I was at the point of killing one of them. I was in a state of total exhaustion caused by anguish. Luckily Michel was bright enough not to give in completely. I'm almost certain that nothing happened between them . . ."

Is he aware of the gravity of his words, of their specific gravity, of what they involve? He keeps on in the same muffled voice, concentrated, tense: "You knew who I was even before you read those notes. Didn't you? From a sexual point of view? They held no surprises for you?"

When I told him that I was rereading *Si le Grain ne meurt*, he gave me the following information: "Du Bos maintained that the whole first part was an unnecessary bore. He refused to understand that I only wrote this beginning to foreshadow the revelations of the last section. I wished to demonstrate how normal and ordinary a foundation my extraordinary youth rested on. That monster whom everyone was surprised at, he too had had an education as bourgeois and natural as any . . ." I was on the point of exclaiming, "There could be nothing as unnatural as your childhood, as your puritanical adolescence!" But I thought it wiser not to interrupt. Then we got on to the subject of the book I'm writing about Cocteau. "I believe you will be able to deliver an excellent study," he said. "I think you are strong enough to resist the dangers of Cocteau's vicinity." And when I exclaimed, "I think so too!" we had this dialogue:

A.G.: Claude, have you ever done anything—how shall I put it?—yes, anything bad, I mean, some imprudent action, something you've regretted afterwards, but which all the same—how shall we say—now then, all the same took you out of yourself?

C.M.: You are touching on an extremely sensitive point with me . . . I am reasonable to the point of a compulsion!

A.G.: Indeed. It was the logic which struck me above all in your articles for *La Flèche*. I am full of admiration for a young man of your age with such self-mastery, such equilibrium . . .

C.M.: Believe me, there is nothing to admire. I suffer from this inability to feel passionately about anything

. . . I am reduced to understanding the loves of other people, completely, but from the outside, and no passion so insane . . . But to never feel anything myself . . .

A.G.: That's very odd . . .

C.M.: And sad. If you were to ask me for a confession, I would dig through my whole past in vain without finding the least imprudence, nothing either very bad, or very good, instead, logical coldness, then as now.

A.G.: Ah, I can see that it is a weakness as well as a strength . . .

We go to lunch. Dismal enough conversation on criticism. When I complained that's all I am, a critic, and nothing else, he sang the praises of critics—he considers them the equals of artists. "They too create . . ." He spoke of Sainte-Beuve whose *Port-Royale* is as fine as the greatest poem, but whom he accuses of treating Ronsard in an offhand manner. A little restaurant off the Boulevard Saint Germain on the Rue Saint Guillaume awaits us. He has admiration for Jean-Paul Sartre. He speaks too of Georges Duhamel, of Malraux.

Back in the Rue Vaneau. The conversation lapses. At last I am free from embarrassment: silences no longer hang over me. Then while Gide takes a nap in the next room, I read the *Journal* which accompanies the confession I read the other day, the pages suppressed in the edition about to appear; 1917-1925 with that important year 1918. The plot thickens. One day Madeleine seeks to free herself from his domination by burning all the letters she ever received from him. What a blow she struck: these letters since their childhood had received the best of his tenderness, and he had counted on them to justify him before society and to justify her, too, by showing what she had meant to him, and the level of morality and intellect their attachment reached. The destruction of these letters had made him smaller, forever: no one now would ever penetrate into his reality. His life would remain a symphony from which an essential part of the score was missing, an unfinished building.

He cries. His wife pretends she doesn't see it: by acting as though she no longer loves him she expects to free him from her and thus her from him. But his love only increases. Yet he realizes that he can never please Madeleine but by renouncing the most basic layers of his nature, by ceasing to be himself. He loves her nonetheless for knowing this. But she doesn't see this. She refuses to see it. Poetry? Music? She has no interests any longer. Because she only loved them in him—and she loves me no longer, he thought at first. Then years later with more penetration: Because I love them. Afraid of discovering him in these realms she closes them to herself. And Gide writes that it was *Les Faux-Monnayeurs* where for the first time in writing a book he was not compelled by a desire to explain himself to her, to persuade her, to give her the information necessary for judging him equitably. (But what about *Les Caves?*)

I finish. Gide returns: I stammer out a few words and make off. He calls me back so I can read an insignificant letter from Jef Last about his friends in the International Brigade—"significant" enough, I guess, but my heart is elsewhere . . .

Outside I phone Father the good news: Gide is coming.

Thursday / June 1, 1939

Leafing through the enormous book that Jean Pierre Maxence has just published, *Histoire de Dix Ans* (*1927-1937*), I ran across a citation of that passage of Marcel Arland that has occupied Gide and myself so often these last weeks: "In the works of André Gide I find a tremendous lacuna and it is perhaps this lacuna which in the end has provoked all my resistance. This work seems unaware of misery . . . All Gide's intellect, intuition and goodness, that true goodness I'm certain I find in him, are unable to fill in for this emptiness which only an understanding of misery could have filled, if he had been willing to learn her lessons."* I was astonished by the catholicity of Maxence, whom I had identified too quickly with B.'s party because of his prejudices in certain matters and his work in the magazine *Gringoire*. Maxence adds this commentary, much to his honor: "Two hours of conversation, free and easy conversation, were enough to reveal to me that certain accusations can no longer be leveled at André Gide—I will not allow it. To tax this man with duplicity is nothing but a sign that one has failed to understand him and that nothing further is possible to make one understand! I know very few '*maîtres*' who impress by their charming restraint, by an exquisite moderation in their statements, by such care not to bear down too hard on the ideas of their

* *Essais Critiques.*

82

partner, so as not to cramp his style . . . One can not without either blindness or dishonesty question the good sense or the worth of this man, or his quality." But all the same he agrees with Arland. Here the question is one of misunderstanding and especially of disagreement on the meaning of a word. Neither Arland nor Maxence would deny that Gide knows what misery is; they only reproach him for not making this the center of his work and of his teaching.

And now a few quotations to shore up the picture of Gide my visits have given me. First of all these lines from *Si le Grain ne meurt*: "To an incredible degree I have lacked, since I can remember, that awareness on which all boldness is founded: the feeling for what I'm worth in the mind of another. I have always aimed so low that, far from merely asking for nothing, when the least favor is shown me I feel so exalted I am unable to disguise my astonishment."

From Roger Martin du Gard this explanation of the ease and lightness I felt on rereading *Si le Grain ne meurt*: "He has a gift for sharpening the critical focus and enlarging the power of self-knowledge which each of us has, and without the usual loss of strength. He does even more: he exalts something I find impossible to define exactly in each of us, not pride certainly, but you might call it an equitable vision of oneself, a modest self-confidence. Some day perhaps I will tell what it means to have a personal talk with André Gide." Up to the present, more than any of our "personal talks," the reading of *Si le Grain ne meurt* has given me this, this cheerfulness.

Last of all Massis has these words which underline that obsession with his own inabilities which Gide confided the other day: "André Gide is not creative . . . No one is more gifted than he in hiding and in justifying his weaknesses. His is not a rich nature."

Paris, Friday / June 2, 1939

Back from Vémars a letter from Maurice Sachs awaited me and I read it with some unwillingness after what Jouhandeau and more than he, Cocteau, has told me: ". . . your book made me want very much to make your acquaintance. We have friends in common among whom are several who have had the time to become my enemies, but rather than ask that one of them introduce us I thought it quicker to write you myself . . ."

When I mentioned this letter to Gide, he must have guessed from my tone of voice how little I thought of its author on the basis of what people have told me because he exclaimed, "I do not in the least look down on this man!" Then he spoke to me with real kindness, better: charity, which disturbed me. Concerning the theft which Cocteau accuses him of, Gide knows nothing. All he knows is that after thousands of mistakes Sachs, distressed and desperate, has tried to make another reputation for himself. He had come to see Gide but because of what he had heard (no details given) Gide received him coolly. But the sincerity of Sachs's repentance touched him. He seemed so unfortunate to Gide that he decided to aid him in the regeneration he wished to effect. It was then that Gide took on Sachs at the *NRF*.

I was touched myself by Gide's tact and the part played in it by a deep charity. To have deserved this, the man must have his nobility. I saw him now as nothing more than an unfortunate being. After that Gide needed very little effort to persuade me to change my mind—I had already decided not to answer the letter.

So I went to Maurice Sachs's place toward the end of the morning. We tramped to La Muette and the Avenue Henri Martin: still very young but a little plump, his stride shortened, slowed down by some invisible sickness, a manner more friendly and honest than anything else, devoid of any semblance of ill will, even, and especially, when he speaks of those who hate him, Jouhandeau and Cocteau.

He tells me that what most made him want to know me was discovering in a person of my age the same admirations that his generation had: Cocteau, Jouhandeau. That surprised him. He would have thought rather that a reaction would have forced us to underrate those who had pleased our elders so. I pointed out that what I like so much in Jouhandeau had been mostly overlooked by his earlier admirers, that I was attracted to the barest pages he has written and condemn totally everything that sent the previous generation into ecstasies, that overdecorated tone of voice, heavy with bad taste and excesses (*Opales*, for instance), all those "nails of gold" which Max Jacob has spoken of and not without praise. The same goes for Cocteau: I disagree completely with all those, Maurice Sachs among them, who were twenty immediately after the War, who say he renovated poetry, the theater and art. All I am interested in is the metaphysical drama of that life haunted by nothingness, and that battle with darkness which I have traced through his entire work. I have judged Jouhandeau and Cocteau with open eyes, something which had been impossible at the time they were discovered because they sparkled too much for any view of them to be the true one. I added that I too might be wrong . . .

Sachs, although he complimented me most extravagantly for my book, seemed after all to seek nothing more in me than the temperature of an epoch and a generation. He questioned me repeatedly but never tactlessly on the influences, the friends, the tastes, the admirations I felt. He too wanted to know what imprudent acts I was capable of . . . And there I was taking him into my confidence just as I had Gide the other day. That is one of my weaknesses: I make my confidences too easily, I am too suddenly direct, too much myself. A posture which seduces with its spontaneity those who find themselves its object. Little do they suspect that the better they know me the less I allow.

Innumerable allusions to his homosexuality. I get bored; I would like to explain to him that the question in my case simply never comes up, that my "imprudences," or rather those acts that I linger over in my mind are of another order altogether. I tell him that with Gide our deepest common ground of understanding is not "sexual freedom" at all but hearts held captive by charity and justice, yet too cowardly to give up the most egotistical and bourgeois of existences.

Friday / June 9, 1939

Today I also had time to run up to Maurice Sachs's before lunch. He had summoned me by telegraph. Now this is surprising. He wants me to edit a review with him! The plan Roger Lannes and I have of editing one ourselves saved me from inventing excuses. He answered with a calm which amazed me: "I am clear-headed enough to know who I am, and more than that to know what I'm said to be. I would understand if a young man refused to compromise himself with anyone as marked as I am, as to morals, as to reputation. I reproach myself, I regret bitterly certain indelicacies . . . I arrange them by weight in my mind . . . I contemplate my excuses, then the lies and exaggerations of my enemies: the debit side is large enough however for me to understand your misgivings . . ." I replied that nothing of that entered into it. I looked him square in the eyes. The first to turn his gaze aside—was me.

Since his return from Cuverville I've tried to reach Gide: I phoned him twice without answer and he called me two times while I was out. Finally this morning I got through to him. He invited me to dinner this evening at the house of Mme. de Lestrange, and unfortunately I'm committed elsewhere. We speak as well of the impediment—temporary it may still be hoped—the difficulty we

87

find ourselves in of finding a cook for our stay at Malagar. Immediately afterwards I receive a long telegram from Gide going over the same ground (he sent it before the call went through that finally allowed us to talk to each other). Here is the best of what he writes: "Your mother tells me that there is uncertainty on the culinary side . . . I had to curtail my stay at Cuverville for reasons of the same order: the little servant we have there was taken to bed brusquely with a sprain. As for myself I hold the end of the month open, just in case. If our beautiful plans for Malagar cannot materialize, so much the worse—I have always shown a penchant for renunciation. And above all don't wear yourself out. But if everything does fall into place, you need do nothing more than let me know in the course of the coming week."

Tuesday / June 13, 1939

At Gide's from 10 to 11:30 A.M. Worked out questions of a practical nature: the sort of clothes to take, suitcases and the rest. Then the wandering Jew himself walks in, expelled from his hermitage at La Celle by Du Bos's return—I mean Denis de Rougemont whom Gide has put up, and his wife too, in that studio of Allegret's. He's in shirt sleeves, his features relaxed as I've never seen them. He repeats his promise to write an article for *La Flèche*. Then, Gide, Rougemont and I discuss the refugee problem. We come to the conclusions that on our modest level it isn't proper for us to be too patient with the government. The government has its duty which is a duty different from ours. In its place we too might find injustices necessary. The public order demands sacrifices. But our role is precisely *not* the government's. Our role is criticism, the prevention of an easy slide into the quickest solutions. Gide is attracted by the idea of our visiting the camps no matter how much André Dubois may be annoyed by this. Another conclusion forced on us is that the Ministry of the Interior is not absolutely free in its handling of the problem—the Police, the Foreign Ministry and the War Department limit its actions and thus our campaign must face all these organizations and not simply inasmuch as they are each responsible, even more inasmuch as in spite of good will they get in each other's way. Whatever my article says Dubois will not have to take offense. It is not he nor precisely the Minister of the Interior who is concerned.

Gide speaks to me about the preface my father has written to Guillemin's book on Flaubert: "This is most serious! The moment they discover that a free-thinker is wise, as soon as they discover that he loves justice and truth, the Catholics annex him . . . But we too have our saints: Littré, Valéry . . . We too are capable of greatness . . . I understand the Catholic position: in possession of the truth they are certain there is no truth but theirs . . . It's the old 'Everything beautiful is French' carried to another plane and the 'She has too much virtue to be anything but a Christian' of Polyeucte. I believe I'm going to answer your father. This is too serious!"

Then he repeats his joy at the prospect of Malagar where all those "suppressed conversations" that he has

89

with my father will flower at last. "Yet I am not, you may well imagine, without a certain uneasiness . . ." He was wearing a sort of black velvet doublet. His cheeks were pale, soiled with a slight growth of beard, sliced by vertical furrows, right and left, his only two wrinkles.

Joyous confusion and clarity in his face showing intimidation and rapture as he calls up the kindness of my parents receiving him with such hospitality. From time to time a distracted quality . . . He tells stories I know already: Péguy calling Dante "that tourist!" Péguy reproached in the name of Christian morality for his severity against Laudet-Le Grix and answering, "I do not *judge*, I condemn!"

Tuesday / June 20, 1939

Dinner at André Dubois's with Lucien Sablé and André Gide. Sablé, who never met Gide before, stammers with emotion. Dubois waited on us hand and foot, so attentive, so open and friendly that he seemed more charming than ever. Gide informs me that "dental bothers" are going to prevent his leaving for Malagar at the same time we do. He'll get there Monday or Tuesday. He discusses his career with a satisfaction that embarrasses me since I prefer him detached and free of vanity: ". . . unknown, or almost, up to my fiftieth year . . . Three hundred copies of my *Nourritures Terrestres* sold in twenty years! That is what is called a failure, failure . . ." etc. Interesting exchange on the subject of my

Cocteau and the way in which I have conceived the problem. Gide says, "It seems to me that you have given in to the pleasure of creating the Jean Cocteau of your dreams . . . The real Cocteau does *not* suffer." To this I replied, "The truth of the matter seems to me as follows: a man named Cocteau who is a remarkable artist heaps up lie after lie in his works. His talents suffice for putting most readers off the scent. And to an unhoped for extent, because they take for jokes the poor smiles with which he hides his misery. No one takes *him* seriously as he wishes they would but they take his acrobatics seriously. And he, who would like to forget that he lies, never is able to forget it completely. Every one of his lies points to the same thing. They aim, every one, at the same target. And for that reason one can see, with a little thought, what they signify. His lies do mean something. They all announce the same thing, the only thing true in Cocteau's heart, his truth. Now his truth is as follows: that death terrifies him, that he cannot believe in the supernatural about which he talks and talks, whose map he pretends to know by heart." 11:30 P.M. We leave. Gide is enchanted by my taking him home in a cab—since Dubois lives almost next door to us while he lives way the devil over on Rue Vaneau.

PART TWO

Malagar

Malagar, Saturday / June 24, 1939

Before we left Paris my father received a note from Gide wishing him *"bon départ, bon voyage et bonne arrivée à Malagar."* Gide added, "I cannot wait to tell you in person how moved I am by your generous proposal that I join you in Malagar—but a cruel dentist has refused me the pleasure of traveling with you.

"What a cry of relief I will give when at last I feel your nearness! I live in the expectation of that moment and remain your friend, André Gide."

At breakfast this morning while the vine twigs scent our beefsteak my father said, "This table we are seated at only dates back to Napoleon III . . . You make the fifth generation of our family that has sat here . . . How fast life goes . . . One life is nothing . . . nothing at all . . ."

The weather is heavy. The vines, the countryside, the houses too look sullen. Walked as far as Verdelais. I told my father how startled I was by a passage in Valéry where he shows surprise at religion's denying a man the benefit of his earlier good deeds if he dies in sin, while from the man who dies repentant the weight of his

95

former sins is removed. Of these two the one is saved while the other is damned. But the life of one is the life of the other—in reverse. And since for God, Time does not exist, Valéry is shocked—my father too. "Who will take upon himself the prediction of the sentence God is going to pass! Valéry may be excused. But very often Christians put this question and forget that the whole Gospel demonstrates that man's justice and God's differ completely. Only a theologian would decide that one is saved, the other lost. We can know nothing about it . . . The only question remains: Does God exist? Does love exist? I can understand that a person can ask questions about that. But if God does exist what importance have our poor thoughts about him? There is nothing for it but to give oneself wholeheartedly to him. We cannot be disappointed. God is love."

And as we arrived at the basilica he said, "Let's go in and pay Him a short visit." And we did so. No faith in me whatsoever, but much good will. I gave myself, with open heart, no other prayer than my silence . . .

Then we went to see the several hundred women and children, refugees from Spain, housed in Verdelais. The wine wholesaler who lets them use his warehouses acted as our guide. Rhetorical, pharisaical, very much of a Rightist if not very righteous, yet absolutely certain that Franco is absolutely "pure"—"Perhaps he was a bit extreme . . ." A bit . . . He tells us that his charges are all hostile to Christianity. "How could it be otherwise?" my father sadly confesses. "They identify it with Franco. Franco is responsible for millions of Spaniards believing Christ is Public Enemy Number One . . ."

The premises were clean, the faces looked healthy and well-fed. Caught sight of several girls magnificent enough to dream about.

Sunday / June 25, 1939

Gide, powerless to invent? I'm rereading *Les Faux-Monnayeurs* in old copies of the *NRF* (unfortunately not a complete set) and I'm surprised to find at the same time so little power of invention and so much detail *remembered.* There is little doubt of the importance played in the "novel" by a real journal. André Gide always shows a real inability to imagine things, or at least of carrying to its final consequences a business whose first idea he has invented. Thus the personality of Bernard is complete from the start and only develops at the expense of his own truth and to the advantage of Gide's truth.

In the person of Passavant I recognize certain traits of our friend Cocteau. More than that, the secrets which Gide blurted out the other day about him give me keys to the relationship between Passavant and Edouard in the novel. Olivier is Michel, of course. Everything Gide admitted to me I find here, hardly transformed at all. Often even the words that I had from his very mouth the other day when he talked about the jealousy he suffered. I quote *Les Faux-Monnayeurs* (check my journal for Wednesday, May 31, 1939): "Everything

97

Olivier told, with such self-satisfaction, about Robert, had the effect of infuriating Bernard and making Robert an object of hate . . .

"Bernard mumbled 'What do you think of the Count de Passavant?'

" 'Good lord, you can imagine can't you?' Edouard said. Then a moment later: 'And you?'

" 'Me?' said Bernard savagely, '*I'd kill him!*' (The change is hardly significant: in reality it is Edouard-Gide who thinks this statement.)

Then these further particulars: "Edouard was in love with Olivier. What pains he would have taken to bring the boy to maturity. What loving respect he would have used to guide him, guard him, bring him—to him. *Passavant will surely ruin him!* Nothing could be more disastrous for him than this unscrupulous encirclement! I would have expected Olivier to have been able to take better care of himself, but he has a tender side that is sensible to flattery . . ."

And of Passavant-Cocteau he writes, "No one can be more injurious or applauded than people of his type."

The character of Laura doesn't seem as closely drawn from life—or I lack the key. But Gide does express himself about her in many of the same sentences which I have heard him apply to his wife. Thus, "She never was able to explain to herself the coldness of her lover; she made herself responsible for it, telling herself that she would have won him if she had been more beautiful, if only she had been bolder: never achieving a real loathing for him, she accused herself, underrated herself, denied herself any importance, and rid herself of her very *raison d'être,* and no longer found in herself any virtue whatsoever." And this note too, doesn't it call up the Madeleine I discovered in Gide's notebook? "In the proportion in which a soul penetrates into the depths of devotion, just so much will it lose the sense, taste, need and love of reality . . . The dazzlement of their faith blinds them to the world around them and to their very selves. For a person like myself to whom nothing means more than clear vision I cannot but remain dumfounded before the density of falsehood in which the pious can take pleasure." Of Laura again, these essential lines from Edouard's *Journal,* which I can almost hear Gide saying to me as he spoke of his relations with his wife: "Laura never seems to suspect her powers, for a moment; but I, as I penetrate deeper into the secret places of my heart, I come to see that to this very day *there is not a single line I have written that she hasn't inspired at least indirectly . . . All the fluency my conversation has I owe to nothing but the desire to be continually teaching her, persuading her, seducing her. I see nothing, I hear nothing I don't think immediately: What will she say?* If she weren't there to make me more precise, my own personality would flow vaguely into the indefinite; I am not even myself nor anything at all except in her presence . . . Involuntarily, unconsciously, each of two beings who love one another changes himself according to the demands of the other and labors to resemble that idol set up for contemplation in the other's heart. *Whoever loves truly renounces sincerity.*

"Thus she threw me off the track. Her thoughts accompanied mine everywhere. *I admired her taste, her intellectual curiosity, her culture, without realizing that only her love of me made her passionately concerned*

99

with all that she saw me taken with. No, she was totally unable to make discoveries for herself. Each of her enthusiasms, I see this today, was nothing more than an afternoon nap where her thoughts could stretch out alongside mine. Nothing in all that answered to any demands of her own nature. 'I dress and put on jewels for none but you,' she would say . . . But of that which she added to herself in order to please me nothing will remain . . . A day comes when the true nature reappears, which time has undressed, removing borrowed finery . . .'' This is very close to the idea which Gide, disappointed, entertained of his wife during a certain period. Later one recalls, and in his *Journal* itself, he expresses reservations to this judgment.

And I shall copy down too this trait of his character: "A singular incapacity for gauging his importance in the heart and mind of others." I have quoted an analogous passage from *Si le Grain ne meurt.*

Monday / June 26, 1939

Fine conversation with my father. We discussed Barrès. "Boredom always stops me after ten pages no matter where I begin. Gide told me the other night at André Dubois' something that surprised me because I thought he liked Barrès and had even recommended him to me: he said, 'Oh I'm not at all surprised that you feel that way . . .' He even looked rather pleased with himself . . ." My father answered, "One of the keys to Gide is his position anti-Barrès. Gide was actuated for a long time

simply by the necessity of saying the opposite of anything Barrès said. Thus he said, 'Families, I detest you
all.' As for what I think of Barrès, I feel a tremendous
gratitude. He was truly a *maître*."

C.M.: That is easily believed. Still a work like his cannot separate itself from the period in which it was conceived. Each page of Barrès answered your own questions while my generation hears nothing there to which
it can pay attention . . .

F.M.: Yes. But there is one thing you must remember:
what a spoiled child *you* were! Up to your neck in excitement, petted, entertained . . . But my childhood, on
the other hand, suffocated in a provincial small town
where my pride—and it was gigantic!—suffered continual wounding, where I saw no one like myself. There
was Lacaze, who was a kind of monster, and I believed
myself a monster, too. How I suffered . . . How sad to
think that at that adorable age—

And he winced, then mumbled, "No, I'd rather not
think about that. So much stupidity makes me sick at
the stomach. And since it is over and done with forever
. . ." It strikes me again what he said the other day about
the novel by Bruno Guy-Lussac: "He describes a young
man, tortured, unfortunate, crazy, sick . . . And it is
obvious that he has poured himself body and soul into
creating this character—or thought that's what he was
doing, which is worse. But the author himself radiates
youth and beauty. Out of ignorance he allows all these
marvels to go to waste . . ." But he returned to the
subject: "Then along came Barrès. Can you imagine the
importance of what he brought me? A *raison d'être?* A
posture for facing life? I was eighteen. I wanted to keep

existence at arm's length, impose an order upon it. Barrès offered me a complete *Ethics*. Look, the very title had me in raptures; this title saved me from scorn which I felt all about me: *Sous l'oeil des Barbares* . . . I would show you, if the book were here, those few splendid pages, ones I used to know by heart."

Then we spoke of Jacques Rivière. My father tells me that at first he was looked down on by Rivière, who felt a poor boy's disdain for the pampered son of wealthy bourgeois parents. "But we caught up with each other during his last years. We began to see each other all the time. When he saw the last of my books which he could have read, *Le Désert de l'Amour,* he told me—I have Drieu la Rochelle as a witness, Rue de la Pompe, several days before Rivière died but he was already gravely ill—'Now that's the novel I would like to have written!' He was *the* critical genius of his generation. Intelligent to excess and above all enthusiastic. It is absolutely necessary to believe what you say. Now as far as he was concerned nothing existed that had more precision or importance than literature. A work meant something to him and he took it seriously. The least page, the least line seemed to him to answer to some essential activity of the man. What a difference: the critics of today, today's tired novels, people who write simply because they're 'writers.' Moreover, Rivière was his generation's *witness*. He mirrored, he catalogued. Nothing got by him unnoticed . . . I loved him very much, even his face which your mother, for instance, finds unattractive—those extraordinarily limpid eyes of his; yes, he had a strange beauty . . ."

Walk at the end of day. A beautiful summer evening.

The gardens fall apart in roses and the trees with cherries. A belated cuckoo calls. My father lauds the country's peace, its beauty.

After dinner I began *l'Education Sentimentale* once more. Beautiful. But what despair I felt when I turned out the light. I owe this despair to Flaubert's novel although the cause is hardly literary: his evocation of the beautiful love affairs possible in the 1840's saddens me now that the possibility has disappeared. I remember all those worlds sleeping now eternally: the court of François I, the court of Louis Philippe, every younger generation since the foundation of the world . . . I remember the tremendous silence that covers these passionate throngs. So much joy, so much love, so much sorrow all ending in this forgetfulness which menaces, equally, my sorrow, my love, my joy. Lassitude. The feeling of, "To what end?" The nothingness of human life, that oft-told tale, suddenly grasps *me* with all its meaning! I went to bed sadly, seeing myself making these sorry movements. How strange. I didn't recognize myself at all. That young unknown interests me no longer. He ought to die before he accomplishes anything. That young unknown —he's me and his unconscious fatuity suddenly appalls me. Tomorrow: Gide.

Tuesday / June 27, 1939

Involved letter in which old complicated Gide decided the hour his train reaches Bordeaux—then telegraphed us a new timetable. In his note he writes (and the . . .'s betray their author), "You will receive this letter early enough to knock me off my feet by telegraph if a catastrophic obstacle . . . Our plan seems so wonderful that I won't believe in its reality until we're together."

After the floor of his room was scrubbed we brought in roses. I looked after paper and ink and books—Balzac and Simenon. Then, long before it was necessary, my father and I left for Bordeaux. We give each other conspiratorial smiles, exchange jokes, imitate him without malice, show our astonishment, indeed, that André Gide really is coming to Malagar, that the adventure of which we talked so long is finally being realized.

He appears in a somber costume, his familiar profile surmounted by the usual wide-brimmed hat. His features scarcely drawn or soiled at all by the trip, but very pale. He gets in the back with my father. I'm up front. Radiant evening transfigures the road. I listen to them chat about an article Claudel just published in *Figaro littéraire* about Maritain. There Claudel writes of the necessity for the Christian of restricting himself to doing his "duties as a citizen . . . without attempting vain and awkward revolutions". . . My father tells Gide that by way of R. P. Maydieu he has learned that Maritain feels very hurt. He adds that as far as he's concerned himself he owes Claudel too much, that light of his youth, that because of the heart in his chest he cannot get what he thinks off his chest . . . But he's surprised that no one has come to the defense of the beautiful little truth which Maritain enunciated: *As long as modern societies secrete misery as a normal product of their operation there will be no rest for a Christian!* Gide is reminded of a statement of de Rougemont's that startled him: How only those countries that have been infected with Christianity ever produce a revolution. My father mentions Mounier. He says that a true revolutionary can only fight for a Christian order . . .

The first thing we did on arriving in Malagar was take Gide to the terrace. The sun was going down, and washed "our view" in the first shadows with here and there a pool of light still trembling. Then dinner. Then on the terrace in an adorable moonlight we enjoyed a quiet conversation. Gide and my father astonished me by knowing so much verse by heart—and knowing the same lines! They recited at little more than a whisper, addressing only each other, sometimes in unison. My father attempted a rehabilitation of the indefensible Sully-Prudhomme: "He is indefensible but all the same he's a poet . . ." In the end Gide agreed. He too quotes, in answer to my father, several lovely lines which he finds such. He has on hat and cape. The night is so gentle, hardly chilly at all and the frogs and crickets fill it with their songs. "You aren't cold?"

"No, I have my cloak . . ."

"Be careful you don't take sick . . ."

"Yes, of course . . . I am a bit weak in the bronchial tubes . . ."

I stare at our three shadows motionless on the gravel. My own looks like an Egyptian statue because I sat down like a gun dog on the parapet of the terrace, profile. My father's lacks definition. Then that dumpy collection, the shadows of André Gide. Of Gide who's saying, "I am a bit weak in the bronchial tubes . . ." It strikes me that this is the same man and the same delicate bronchial tubes that visited Biskra during a voyage a long time ago, known to everybody nowadays, and how then, sick, he could not surrender to life, his life . . .

A funny life! But I thought of the words of my uncle the *abbé,* so justly spoken the other evening: "Gide has been able to make the worst secrets of his sexual life public. And nonetheless he is correctly considered a *moraliste.* The sincerity of his position and the courage he has shown (in particular about the USSR) gave him a tremendous prestige which he merits, yes, he does." What importance and grandeur he has indeed in my eyes. "The miracle is that he also affected the boys of my generation with the same hypnotic power," says my father.

The Maritain affair came up again. How Gide loathes Claudel! He says without a smile that Claudel is M. Couture exactly—without the lubricity. He returns without seeming to ever tire of it to another idea which seems to fill him with comfort: "There is a whole party of Catholics who have taken up cudgels against you, Mauriac—Massis, Claudel and their followers; they all claim you're a heretic—and simply because you do have charity and nobility." My father answers that it isn't happening, that it's already happened: there is a new heresy called Supernaturalism. But he has been informed that any attempt to press charges would meet with "the personal friendship with which His Holiness regards you"—"Friendship, by the way, which you share with Generalissimo Franco," I said. Then turning to Gide: "Why, Monsieur Gide, don't you write that article yourself? The prestige surrounding the name Claudel, the friendship and thanks so many owe him prevent many men, my father among them, from taking up their pens. But you, now there's nothing to stop you . . ."

"I've thought of it . . . But I'm afraid—of compromising Maritain!" His face suddenly lights up with pride and humility. A triumphant irony twists his features and gives them, gives them a touch of comedy and a suggestion, oh, only a suggestion, of the demoniacal. He goes on: "There you are! They'll say, 'But of course! Look who's defending Maritain; Gide! That figures . . . Poor Maritain . . . etc.' And in the same way you too will be compromised by my presence here, François Mauriac. Oh yes! 'And who was it, it was François Mauriac, of course, who has taken Gide in as a boarder . . .'" There again I hear Gide's paranoia, so painful, caused by the wounds never healing under the continual insults, snubs, intentional misunderstanding. He has some of that manner the old dog has; grateful, overcome, dumfounded, old dog that expected a beating and received a kind hand instead.

The night was so gentle that we stayed out later than usual. Gide tells us about the British Academy's removing him from its list of members (he replaced Anatole France) when it became known that he'd joined the Communist Party. And now they're trying to make up by suggesting a banquet in his honor! He also rehearsed the amusing story which follows: Just after an issue of the *NRF* appeared, Gide saw it pulled from the handbag of an old lady who had sat down across from him in a train. She began to read. Touched, Gide began, "Excuse me, Madame, but I see that you are a reader of a magazine that is very close to my heart. In fact I believe you may be reading something by me at this very moment . . ."

Then, stammering with joy, and overcome, she, whoever she was, got up, and so teary that she appeared to be on the point of falling on her knees, she cried "You! It is you! What happiness! Oh it is you in very truth Monsieur Duhamel!"

Wednesday / June 28, 1939

In Langon on errands, alone with Gide. He finds something interesting in everything, picking out hundreds of exciting details in even this dull town. An admirable curiosity: he wants to see everything—even things ugly. Nothing gets by him. The Rue Maubec charms him— with its windows full of unspeakable *objets d'art*. He is astonished there how people's desire for the beautiful goes astray.

In a store filled with the incense of roasting coffee he spots a young Annamese. He points him out to me and overwhelms me with questions: how is it that an Annamese is here and so on . . . A few minutes later the boy passes us and enters another shop. Gide stops, looks, starts, turns to look over his shoulder and walks on regretfully. Then he says, "What a shame! Had I been abroad I'd have spoken to him. He'd have seen nothing odd in my speaking. While in France and speaking French to a Frenchman . . . At Cuverville I never go to the village because everyone knows me by sight and I can't stand it. But *even here* I don't dare make the acquaintance of a young Annamese and ask him to a bar—something that would be very easy in the East . . ."

I don't say a word. But I believe Gide wouldn't be identified here. Yesterday on the way back from Bordeaux we stopped here at the station to pick up his trunk. I watched that man in black who spoke with my father. Travelers passed them, indifferent travelers who probably took him for a lawyer or a justice of the peace. I felt a slight discomfort.

Again I will be spending too much of my time on this journal. And I will miss it since right now I really have a mind to do my Cocteau. I'm giving my mornings to this journal and saving the afternoons for real work. But meanwhile there has been lunch and a lunch at which my father and Gide touched grave subjects indeed—so I must rearrange my time. *La Vérité du Mensonge* can wait. *Truth of the Lie?* The other night at André Dubois' Gide discussed with me my previous title (but how could he have known it?) *Précisions sur l'Enfer.* Last night he repeated how happy an idea he found it and I explained that it was a title I was saving for some other occasion since Jean Cocteau appeared on closer examination to be unworthy of it, I mean initiated into no variety whatsoever of the supernatural, and Gide exclaimed "Exact-ly! Show how and why he remains outside Hell. But what would that particular demonstration consist in if not *précisions sur l'enfer?*"

My insufficiencies strike me as soon as I hear my father and Gide chatter away. I feel myself to be subtle enough in my own realm but how narrow it is! Very quickly I lose the thread. Then I suffer with the knowledge that I am not worthy of my good fortune: sitting between André Gide and François Mauriac. But I do have enough intelligence in this non-intelligence to take the measure of my deficiency. I know exactly the point at which I must give up. There is nothing before me then but shadows in which I glimpse my father and Gide disappear with the confidence of nocturnal birds. And if I am confused as to the shapes of things by the sur-rounding fog I can still imagine their significations. I even feel that with a bit less laziness and a little more self-confidence I would be able to re-create what is not given to me, that is to say, conquer with difficulty but victoriously a domain which has heretofore been closed to me. Thus it would be possible after all for me to attain something through perseverance which other in-telligences, ones that are greater, naturally receive.

These thoughts came to me after lunch, in the salon, over coffee as Gide and my father discussed Christianity. I could perceive that in the banal disguise of their con-versation the deepest and most delicate points were being raised by each of them and I thought, "If only Maritain were here, or Du Bos, how quickly these sen-tences would become weighty . . ."

As for me, what position remained? The uneasiness which Gide brought to the surface at the mention of the disappointing narrowness of spirit—or better: the dis-appointing malice on the part of most Catholics. My father's act of faith: mere human beings have no importance, nor what they have made of Revelation, not even the Church, for that matter, inasmuch as it too is an institution of men and a prey to every sickness of the social organism. Only Christ's reality, His existence, matters. Catholics are especially disappointing since they have a mission given them which they appear, almost to a man, to be unworthy of. No different from other men, they are worse in the sense that their faith should have raised them higher. Yet one must not attempt to pass judgment on God simply from the stammered testimonies of his servants. On the subject of the *Flaubert* by Guillemin with my father's preface, Gide posed a serious problem: Is there no holiness outside the Faith? My father answered him with a parable which seemed to astonish our guest and fill him with a rather definite satisfaction. "A woman of great simplicity but who almost reaches the level of sainthood said of a friend of mine who had remained an agnostic, 'On her deathbed she was obsessed by the idea, a real thirst, of joining the Church. I feel that such an action would have been mere weakness on her part, an abdication, and that God must prefer her courage, her strength of character, her uprightness which right up to her last gasp prevented her from giving in to the gentle temptation of eternity. A person who is without faith should not give in to his fear and believe or make an appearance of believing simply to find help.' Those were the words of this saintly woman. Everything is a question of type. In the realm of grace there are only individual cases. On the other hand there are others who refuse to believe and in so doing betray themselves and betray God. Those are the ones who make a truly grave mistake . . ."

Gide interrupted: "And me. What have I ever done but refused to give myself . . ."

"From insufficient faith—or from its opposite, a fear of having to surrender to one's faith and what that faith demands, the way Julien Green did—at least so it appears, because, of course, we can only judge from appearances."

Gide answered, "Yes and no. For both those reasons." There was a silence and then he continued; "Yes, in this realm there are only individual cases . . . More and more I find myself unable to pass judgment on my fellow men."

"And you are right," my father summed up, "because *one never knows* and one cannot know the ways of God."

This morning at breakfast while I detailed a dream of mine of the night before, I suddenly saw Gide with a sort of vertigo! His wife had already died, and he was seventy, in spite of that youthfulness of body and feature. And didn't I surprise him this very morning on the floor of the hall doing his exercises and with the ease of a much younger man? He hardly appeared the least bit out of breath when he got up. Everything is behind him and everything is before me: that surprised me, even shocked me, I have such a settled feeling of our being on exactly the same level in regard to existence and religion.

This afternoon there was *"quartier libre."* Gide took a nap, I wrote my journal, my father worked on his book. We came together again at five. Although this is not part of our routine, we discovered that a little tea, some toast and jam are not disagreeable to our guest, who appears very fond of his food. (The meals here have pleased us in quantity as well as quality.) Then we took a drive. Bazas with its almost oriental atmosphere: gloomy little streets, whitewashed houses like those anywhere around the Mediterranean, even its most distant shores. Uzets. That curiosity and endless good will which Gide evinces, whenever there is anything to see and to understand, found much employment. The late afternoon was beautiful. I drove very slowly so that he wouldn't miss the light on the pine trees' tawny trunks, on the small steers of the Bazadais. And in the rear-view mirror I caught sight of that close-shaven face, eroded, or rather: polished, and worn, and stretched.

After dinner the moon little by little covered the court-yard. Through the salon window music pours, noble, moving, perhaps Bach. The contrasting calm of the night allowed it its full meaning. As day ended Gide had frolicked like a schoolboy and with a schoolboy's lightheartedness when he spotted a June bug. That insect never reaches his part of the country; how happy he would have been to own one in the old days when he collected coleoptera! Night had completely fallen but the moonlight gave it life. With something close to pigheadedness Gide insisted on discussing religion again. He kept leading the conversation back to it and did so from the most distant points. And he is rather defensive and even obsessive. He seems to suspect my father continually of intransigence and Machiavellian tactics. But really, isn't he the one who behaves with intransigence, the one who is—I must allow myself this not very gidian word: a bigot? But isn't the answer that if on occasion Gide acts this way there is real instinct behind it, perhaps because he feels himself too close to faith, almost its tool; thus he fights, fiercely? My father on the other hand can be detached—his faith has a firm basis—and reveal his understanding, and astonish Gide with the broadness of his opinions and thereby topple Gide's arguments beforehand, annoying him.

"But my dear friend," cried my father, "the Catholic Church has never maintained that those who were outside and belonged to another faith were lost! On the contrary. It is possible to be outside the body of the Church and participate in its soul just as it is possible to be a part of that body and never come near the soul."

"That makes me very happy, only too happy," says Gide, dislodged from his position and adopting another strategy. And he adds his habitual, "That's so . . . That's so . . ."

"Just a minute, my friend! You are not a Mohammedan. You are one of us, one of the lambs that has strayed . . ."

"Indeed . . . Indeed . . ." Gide whispers. And he punctuates his silences with his customary nasal sighs.

An aria by Mozart rises through the night. My father maintains there is nothing closer to the supernatural than Mozart. The very existence of such melody renders a materialistic philosophy null. Gide at once tosses in details from the unchristian carryings-on of that composer. He is hardly willing to admit that Mozart was capable of the most heart-rending laments. I feel a certain disappointment. One thought came to reassure me: that he is so susceptible in these matters because they torture him so. "He's afraid," my father said later. "He lacks firmness. His agnosticism seems rather uncomfortable to him. He suspects something is wrong . . . He repeats I am André Gide, yes, I am, and what a responsibility! And he is afraid . . ."

Before going off to our beds Gide and my father exchanged memories of Francis Jammes. Every detail was a pretext for a quotation. Their faithful memories went to it from full hearts. The charm of those easy verses touched me as much when the ecstatic voice of my father murmured them tenderly as when they came to me hammered out, sculpted and detached by our inspired guest.

He got up suddenly and left us "to go meditate a little before sleep." It was still relatively early—10:30. I suspect him of having been forced to take that hurried escape by excessive discretion. Or perhaps he ran off to make a few entries in his *Journal* like "Mauriac must at any price prove that the ancient Greeks are Christians . . ."

Thursday / June 29, 1939

Henri Guillemin spent the day. He was so moved by the presence of André Gide that he barely opened his mouth the entire time he was here. At lunch only Gide and my father spoke. Very intimate conversation . . . Then, at the end, when I gave them my opinion in a word or two, my father cried, "Good lord! You're here too! I'd forgotten you were present . . ." He looked a little embarrassed. But he smiled when he said, "At the time we were discussing just now you were still in 'the unnamed empire of the possible' as our friend Sully-Prudhomme used to say."

"Well, I'll be, you're going to end up by making me accept him too," cried Gide with a laugh. "That's Sully-Prudhomme? But that's rather good!"

From 3:00 to 5:30 my father read his *Mal-Aimés*. Gide let escape his monosyllables, his sighs, his interjections either stupefied or admiring. After the first act he whispered, "One cannot *help* but be captivated." After the second, "It's *fright*ening. What power. What *cru*elty. What complexity." During the reading of the third act (and my father read with real passion), I concentrated on Gide's features: attention, fascination, a contortion that betrayed the proximity of tears. He breathes noisily. All the while, outside, a wagon passes, overflowing with hay. Henri Guillemin, on the edge of his chair, motionless, staring straight ahead, a cigarette gone out in one hand a little way from his lips. Suddenly his fingers rush in under his glasses to wipe away a tear. That's all. Guillemin would burst into tears if he were to open his mouth. Gide can do no more than throw out a few short words of praise. He is able to do nothing more than squeeze my father's hand very hard and whisper, "It's overpowering, that's so, that's so . . . I am very moved . . ." My father gazes on his work with pleasure. Little by little, over the teacups, calm is regained.

Gide no makes no criticisms at all. He proclaimed his total satisfaction. "It is perfect. There isn't a thing that can be changed. But the limits of what an audience can endure have almost been reached. That's so, that's so . . ."

As soon as Guillemin left we got in the car. After a visit to the little church of Saint-Léger we initiated Gide into the charms of the park at Saint-Symphorien, which he enjoyed. Moist heat announcing storms was unable to prevent a touch of mystery, something gliding among the pines, grazing the high-topped bracken. "An appalling atmosphere," says Gide, "yet how appealing!"

"Yes," my father replies, "I believe that it is here that I came to understand what I understand. My work has been what it is because this country is the way it is, suffocating but with what miracles of odor . . ." He began to tell Gide the story of his childhood: "There's the Great Oak which we had surrounded with such a cult that we embraced it last of all before leaving after vacations, my brothers and I . . . There's La Hure on which we launched what we called *boat-lighthouses*—a match stuck in a slice of cork . . ." My own memories welled up: those grand Septembers! But I silenced them: in this place my father alone has the right of remembering . . .

After dinner, in the courtyard, under the linden tree because of a fine rain, my father reads passages, magnificent but unintentionally funny, from Du Bos' journal. How true it is that all it requires is an ironic look for the most beautiful things to fall flat . . . But Du Bos is only too vulnerable on this account. Gide's fresh laughter. The laughter of a young man. Pure. I have the feeling that now I see him for the first time *as he is.*

117

That for the first time he is not watching himself, holding himself back.

Then a conversation in the salon: Gide tells us story after story about the first postwar numbers of the *NRF*—I go looking for them—and about his correspondence with Martin du Gard and more . . . His admirable conscientiousness has him turn on Radio Paris for a trial broadcast which he must judge since he's a member of the National Broadcasting Council: a lovely voice quotes some Edgar Quinet.

Then a curious conversation about Musset took place. In the name of his former admiration for this poet my father attempted to measure out his praise. He made so able a defense, chose his quotations so well that little by little Gide changed his mind. He began to recite too. A concert for two began. They came to the conclusion that in spite of obvious weakness there was real poetry here that was worthy of their love in the old days. Gide asked, "And what does our Claude think?" "Nothing, of course," replied my father with his polite irony, "the little barbarian!"

And as long as one quotation gave rise to another, gushing from one memory to the other, I felt a certain shame.

Friday / June 30, 1939

Gide came down at 9:30 in an unbelievable "costume" of burgundy color tailored from a bolt of material presented to him in the Soviet Union. And he admitted to being uncertain whether he should let us see it and only did so timidly. We were alone, just the two of us, since my father had not yet come down. First we made conversation. But all of a sudden he began to speak to me, his head turned, his whole body at an angle to me—and I recognized the posture of his unguarded moments of self-confident confidences. "If you only knew the self-revulsion I feel sometimes, Claude. I have in me a need of sympathy, friendship that carries me to the very boundaries of hypocrisy. No, that word is not too strong! Nor would the word: perfidy!" A silence, then, "How difficult all this is to say." Silence. I come out with something or other to give him further courage. Then he whispers, "Would you like an example of this inadmissible weakness? The way I gave in last night arguing with your father about de Musset. Overcome by a need for agreement, by a thirst for concord . . . How I did reproach myself for cowardice once I was in my bed!"

"But de Musset, sir, that's nothing important! You were obliged to do nothing *essential,* just to recognize rightly or wrongly that de Musset is a true poet."

"Of course. But that example was just one from many, many of them more serious. You tell me of my 'fame,' of my 'grandeur.' But I know the less 'important' sides of myself . . . I pass judgment on myself —and my cruelty sometimes leaves me breathless . . . I can no longer allow myself the benefits of various doubts. Everything in me appears to deserve condemnation. And I am always under the impression that I have just told a lie. Often I find myself mouthing trivialities, anything that comes into my head—just to escape from myself . . ."

"I have to admit that you gave me a surprise yesterday when you maintained that in her art Spain has never known beauty."

"Oh, I merely expressed myself badly! No, I didn't dare try. I have written several pages in which I explain myself with perfect clarity on this point: Spain could not know beauty because Helen did not land there . . . But I suffer from the emptiness that follows on the exposition of my thought and can only quote myself if I were to attempt further explanation. Unspeakable to be reduced to this, to have known and expressed already all that one is able to know and express! Is there any worse stupidity, anything more laughable than quoting oneself? Now to avoid that I am willing to say almost anything . . ."

"Something that amazes me when you and my father talk religion is the importance you attach to the little things. I'll be quite open with you: for me the important thing is to have a yes or no answer to the question, Does God exist and is the soul immortal? And whatever the answers are, the rest makes no difference at all. Nothing seems less important to me than orthodoxies and that there could have ever been 'Wars of Religion' astounds me. Everything boils down to belief—or disbelief . . ."

"I agree completely," Gide cries, "and I know what my answer is: *I do not believe, I know there are no grounds for belief, of that I am certain!*" He spoke his lines with fire, at the trumpet pitch of a confession of faith.

"But all the same, what anguish!"

"Really? I assure you I now feel a minimum of anguish. My model remains Goethe."

"But Goethe, at night in his bed may have been eaten up with anguish. What was left of his famous 'peace' then? And you, sir, and me . . . I have read many a heart-rending page of Valéry on this subject: his certainty of non-existence . . ."

"Ah . . . How many hours of discouragement and hopelessness I owe to Valéry's companionship . . . At your age I was still very religious, you know. I still have something left from those days. Valéry's negativisim used to dismay me, still does."

At that moment my father walked in. We talked about the note on Claudel which *Temps Présent* had just published. Then we went for a walk. The tomb of Toulouse-Lautrec, the basilica of Verdelais, and the camp for refugees: about fifty children were gathered in a barn where a young man heard their lessons. A former professor of law with a handsome face. Gide shows a polite interest. Before long though he is moved. We watch these children with something like terror, most of them so beautiful, both the boys and the girls. We think of the tragedy they have lived through before war left them in this village, high and dry, in exile. The teacher and his wife, and two other households of teachers and nurses receive us. What an open way they have with us, so upright, marvelous! In front of Gide, overpowered, in front of my father, in front of the *sous-préfet* of Langon, attracted by the importance of these visitors, they discuss with simplicity the misery that's behind them, their day-to-day existence here, their hope of a speedy departure: Santo Domingo awaits them and a peaceful existence down there. "The time has come to start one's life over . . . We are tired, so tired . . ."

They go into details of the war, their flight, the present misery of Spain. They know the names Gide and Mauriac. "We are friends, you know . . . We like Spaniards—not all of them, of course," my father says. He contributes 200 francs for the children. Gide gives as much.

On our way home we stopped in to see Old Suzanne. We have known her happy, but since then her husband has died; she has been exhausting herself taking care of the children she took in. She's had all she can stand. Distress in her tears. My father attempts to calm her. Gide turns away. The two children, awful yet charming, with their really crooked air suddenly look very *worthy*.

After lunch Gide leans on the mantelpiece in the salon, turns his head a little to the side and speaks with a bemused smile of *Les Mal-Aimés*: "Oh, the Devil, you must admit, does get his due. He gains a great deal by this adventure, it cannot be denied!"

My father laughs. He told me later that in that wine-red costume with his cape, the gray one with broad sleeves, our guest appeared to out-gide Gide.

"And your play, my dear Gide?"

"Oh, please don't hold me to my promise that I'd read it to you! It really is too poor . . . I am out of the running now."

"Come on," my father cried, "you know perfectly well that you're well ahead!"

It was easy for us to persuade him and he gave his promise that he would give a reading that very night.

After an interesting conversation about Oscar Wilde and Lord Douglas (which I simply haven't time to go into) he left us. The hour of his daily nap had sounded.

"Which I haven't the time . . ." I mean it. This morning in a letter from Jean Davray I read, "The dialogues of Gide and Mauriac must be peculiar. But if you're playing Eckermann you've hardly time left to work on your Cocteau . . ." If it were simply a question of Cocteau it would be nothing, but I've hardly a minute to read, write, or even live, apart from these hours spent in the presence of Gide. Just keeping this journal eats into my nights.

Gide has several times asked me to let him read my notes on Cocteau. But they are not yet ripe. Instead I gave him the manuscript of my *En deçà de l'Honneur.* He seemed to be touched.

L'Intérêt Général. A play . . . His play . . . What can I say? The reading took place in the study. Introduced, interrupted and continually commented on by its author: "It isn't even finished exactly . . . I'm ashamed to read you this . . . The social orientation spoils it completely . . . Fortunately my books will protect the opinion you have of me . . . Oh, how banal . . . I am *dismayed* . . ." In spite of his admirable voice, which moves one so easily, his embarrassment was such that I was unable to lose myself, and all the more since I saw right away that my father looked severe and dissatisfied and I too felt disappointed. Gide feeling that the air grow thick with hostility, feeling that he had contributed first

123

of all to its birth by means of his reticences, explications, regrets; Gide came finally to not daring to read *all* of it. He skipped whole scenes and at last an entire act.

"You aren't tired?"

"Ah . . . It is worse than that. If it were only a matter of being *tired* . . ."

When it was all over a heavy embarrassment hung over us. My father did not try to save his own skin and with a minimum of polite words, really, explained to Gide that the play wouldn't do, which was the truth, that it presented all the faults (he almost said "all the clichés") of plays of ideas (he almost said "the worst plays of ideas") in which the employer is painted, inevitably, disgusting, while the striking workers come off, inevitably, as angels. How sorry for Gide I felt then and at the same moment admired his bravery. He had words for his play even severer than our own. But such sadness showed through his simulated calm that I felt something like dread.

"How awful it is to grow old," he said. "Whatever one does is less good, so much less good. One knows, but one can't help writing."

"Let it lie for some time in a drawer, that's the best thing to do," advised my father.

"But, my dear friend, I'm already seventy!"

My father makes vague protestations. Then rephrases with an unconscious cruelty in the new precision: "I mean a few *months.* Just a month or two will give you the proper distance you'll need to rework it."

"No, no, no. Better to renounce . . . That's it, that's it . . . I've just gathered commonplaces. For five years now I've been dragging that play around, and it's got to stop!

Robert's character (the employer) is drawn so boldly and the others nuanced so delicately—there's an inadmissible lack of balance right there. And I haven't even read you the more important scenes—out of shame. I haven't even *written* the most important ones. No, what's the use of going on?"

It was truly pathetic to hear him go on like this over our poor protests—which we didn't believe any more than he.

"I have nothing more to say, you know. For a year now I've been on the wrong track. Even my *Journal* has stopped."

"But life does go on . . ."

"Oh, I do try to appear to be alive."

Dinner did a little toward breaking up this crust of embarrassment. As I got up from the table—my father had stepped out of the room for something or other—I ran over to Gide: I felt he had need of a few encouraging words. "You know I have so much to say to you about that play. Seriously, so grand an effort *must not* be wasted. In *Intérêt Général* there are fine passages, and certainly a fire and the breath of life—you've got to save them. You fail perhaps because the subject does not lend itself to dramatic presentation. If that is the case you must begin again at the beginning. You will keep on beginning again until you do find the form demanded by the testimony we await from you. Because it does matter that you should finally have your say on the social situation. Absolutely. All of us are concerned."

In his almost happy face I read real gratitude. "You have given me back my self-confidence. But I have something to say to you about your manuscript . . ."

My father came back. We searched through Racine.
Gide read a passage from *Mithridate,* then my father
recited sublime fragments of *Andromaque.* We ended
with letters of Racine and Boileau in which nothing but
position and money are ever mentioned—and the king,
of whom they stammer with servility. Lackies. Thus
they were treated and so they behaved.

"Horrible age!" I burst out. "Nothing is worth that.
Versailles wasn't worth that. 'The Golden Age' cannot
pay for that!"

But my father demonstrated that our age is even more
revolting, our age threatened with some final annihila-
tion. "Age exciting as well as revolting," says Gide. "I
could not have chosen a different one!" I tell them how
I envied those young Spanish couples this morning; they
have experienced the worst distress, I'll admit, but they
have been saved. I whispered, "I too, I'd leave for Santo
Domingo. In the shade, with a wife, with my books . . ."

Then we broke up for the night. For me, bedtime
deferred for the sake of this journal. Exhausted already,
I'm not at the end of today's account.

"Having arrived at the end of his life," my father
remarked after Gide left us, "he draws a balance. His
faults are clear to him. No longer any way to change the
unalterable total. His wife . . . He's already played his
hand. Finished. I guess he's tormented by remorse. And
I'm fond of him because he's prudent, clear-sighted, and
brave . . ."

But he is astonished that André Gide could write a
play "so totally worthless—resurrects every lousy cliché of
the theater of Antoine!" Moreover, now that the excitement which caused its conception had subsided he

126

hasn't regained his critical faculties: "To think that Gide wrote that, Gide!" He had admitted to us, "I was right in the middle of my honeymoon with Communism when I conceived this." Jouvet had accepted it. The happenings of June 1936 interrupted the staging. Since then he had completely rewritten it—but it is, I fear, a complete loss . . .

I must say in closing how much André Gide means to me *today*. What humanity he has! In sorrow what grandeur!

Saturday / July 1, 1939

Weren't we closer to Racine last night than was Parisian society in disguise honoring him on his tercentenary at a ball Étienne de Beaumont gave? My sisters were among *"les demoiselles de Saint-Cyr."* By the way, Luce wrote our father, "The other day at the Greghs we saw Valéry who asked after Claude with a roguish look. I answered, 'He's at Malagar—with Father.' Valéry smiled maliciously and added, 'And someone else!' I believe he'd very much like to be the fourth."

I had hardly washed when Gide asked me to come to his room. He is concerned very much by letters he receives from refugees at the end of their tether. The whole morning he has forced himself to translate them, write to André Dubois on their behalf and so on. How admirable I find this devotion!

"It's very mysterious," he whispered. "I feel so much closer to you than to your father. And yet he provokes endless admiration, esteem and gratitude in me. It's doubtless all a question of generations. I am so happy to be here. I have so many things to say to him. But I can never forget that it is to you we both of us owe this meeting, that without you it could not have taken place. And that, I'd say that's quite miraculous, that's so, yes . . ."

Then we got onto the subject of his play. I told him that he deceived himself or someone was deceiving him if he thought the suppression of the social aspects of his subject would improve the play. That *is* the subject. To the point that it will be impossible to remove the social aspect and keep the play. And it is precisely this flesh-and-blood problem that we all hope he will come to grips with. But his experiment of the other night proves (and he ought to have foreseen this) that such a subject is not compatible with the stage.

"What I envisage," I added, "is a commentary with which you accompany the critical scenes of your play. In the commentary you would fill in all the subtleties, all the life which the play lacks. That would be something in relation to the theater that *Les Faux-Monnayeurs* is among novels."

The idea seemed to appeal to him. "You're right! That would be magnificent! This play in which I no longer had any interest, this play of which I was sick and tired now excites me once more! A commentary, but of course!" His face lit up, he said, "Then last night's reading *wasn't* a complete waste of time . . ."

At the table, then later over coffee, our conversation was relatively weightless . . . Gide and my father reminisced about Mme. Mühlfeld's salon. Toward the end of the afternoon two of the Spanish families I spoke of the

128

other day paid us a visit. They're still speaking of Santo Domingo. We offered them tea and rivalled one another in being friendly. Then a drive to Castets. We wandered into the courtyard of the castle, so mysteriously beautiful. After dinner Gide and my father had an interesting conversation on Cocteau, Rivière, and the years right after the war . . .

With regard to this conversation (about a detail from the life of Proust that Sachs mentions in the *NRF*, my father said later, "There is no one more courtly, no one more charming, more *amiable* than Gide, and yet suddenly something in him unsticks and he shows himself, just for an instant, as a real demon. For instance, yesterday, leaning with his elbows on the mantlepiece, his back turned, while he talked to me about my play, *Mal-Aimés*. And again, tonight, for instance, about Proust."

Sunday / July 2, 1939

This morning Gide came and sat with me in the courtyard while they did his room. In his hand he held the manuscript of *En deçà de l'Honneur*. A few criticisms of details. Then about prostitution, which I barely mention, he says, "I advise you to cut that passage. You would have to go into it at greater length; as it stands, your remarks are banal. And can you really believe that paying for a pleasure makes it cease to be a pleasure?" Then, "I don't believe we see eye to eye on this subject . . . But certain pages of your pamphlet awoke deep memories in me, that's so, yes . . . I recalled this detail that didn't go into *Si le Grain ne meurt* because it doesn't add to my mother's stature. My mother decided to give Anna Shackleton a dictionary, Anna Shackleton whom I loved for so long much more than I loved my mother—after she moved out of our place I visited her at least once a week—and that was a fine gesture on my mother's part. I don't deny that. But she added these words which hurt me in my heart of hearts because at that moment I discovered for the first time the existence of social injustice and experienced the inhumanity of the bourgeoisie: 'For the likes of her a morocco binding isn't necessary, cloth will do just as well; Anna Shackletons don't know the difference.'" I remembered a passage of *Si le Grain ne meurt* which begins, "Properly speaking, it was as a companion for my mother that Mlle. Shackleton entered our household . . ."

After lunch both of them read aloud in the courtyard: my father read the epistle for today, a veritable oriental lovesong, and that for August 15th, with that voice of his that knows how to give expression to all the poetry in a text, then Gide read passages from the Bible. He reads with a serious voice, vibrant, cruel and gentle, the voice which he doesn't use in conversation nor in the recitation of poems he knows by heart: his reading voice. What overpowers me in it is all the suggestion . . . Gide has managed to pick out the most ambiguous pages in the Bible. He acts out every detail. He completes the silences with a smile, a nod of the head, a gesture. No longer the tenderness of my father, Gide's voice means a shrewdness without mercy, implacable with its hammerings.

First of all, the verses in which the incest of Amnon,

son of David, is narrated. Will I ever be able to forget
the tone of voice? I will underline the words on which
the already overemphatic pronunciation of Gide came
down with extra weight: " 'And it came to pass after
this, that Absalom the son of David had a fair sister,
whose name was *Tamar;* and Amnon the son of David
loved her.' " And these verses especially, from which the
reader was able to coax every overtone, and with what a
disquieting pleasure on his part: " 'Why art thou, being
the king's son, lean from day to day? . . . And Amnon
said unto him, *I love Tamar, my brother Absalom's sis-*
ter. And Jonadab said unto him, Lay thee down on thy
bed, and make thyself sick . . .' " And this bit too:
" '. . . but, being stronger than she, forced her, and lay
with her. Then Amnon *hated* her exc*eed*ingly; so that the
hatred wherewith he hated her was greater than the *love*
wherewith he had loved her . . . And Absalom her
brother said . . . but hold thy peace, my sister: he is thy
brother; *regard not this thing . . .*"

Next he gave us, and with the same accent, totally
lacking in sweetness, and with a sense of mimicry that
brought before us all the duplicity, cruelty and guile of
the dying King David, that terrible passage in which he
gives parting advice to his son Solomon: " '. . . and I
sware to him by the LORD, saying I will not put thee to
death with the sword. Now therefore hold not him
guiltless: . . . but his hoar head bring thou down to the
grave with blood.'

"Can you still maintain, as you did the other day, that
there is no contradiction between the Old Testament
and the New?" Gide cried, excited by the cruelty of
David and finding in that gap between the conceptions

131

of Jehovah and the Saviour a happy augury for his incredulity.

But there again, were there not two Gides fighting in
him for mastery? If he can hunt with such ferocity for
proofs to bolster up his incredulity, isn't it perhaps that
something impedes it, that it is heavy with a nostalgia
for God? And the next passage he read with a voice
which was almost Christian, with emotion, with a
composure in which nothing remained of the delights
which preceded: that pathetic passage in which to save
Sodom, Abraham bargains for it with God: " 'Peradventure there be fifty righteous within the city . . . If I find
in Sodom fifty righteous I will spare all the place for
their sakes . . . Peradventure there shall lack five of the
fifty righteous; wilt thou destroy all the city for the lack of
five?' " And little by little Abraham obtains God's agreement to saving the city if ten just men are found in it.

Gide confessed to placing this text higher than the
most beautiful pages of Greek literature. He was moved,
physically touched by it. He whispered, "Is it that I find
here my childhood to whom these lines were dear? No,
no, it is a question of The Beautiful, isn't it? Of in-
trinsic Beauty." Then he found his most sardonic tone
to read us how when they saw the angels the population
of Sodom desired them *from the very children to the old
men.* Once again the Devil stalks . . .

"I'm going to tell everyone that François Mauriac
forced me to spend a whole Sunday afternoon reading
the Bible," he laughed.

And my father answered, "And I will go into more
detail: Gide chose the most scandalous passages, as is
only right . . ."

Tea brought us together again. André Gide says that Bossuet's *Méditations sur l'Evangile* "casts me automatically into the camp of the unbelievers by reason of his pretensions." I had thought that he was already there . . . Hadn't he told me so? But the human heart isn't that simple, especially André Gide's.

What shall I say of our daily drive? Sauveterre de Guyenne, Blasimon, the little village of Mauriac. More than the romanesque churches which delight Gide and my father so, I am touched by the richness of this landscape which the sun floods and the scent of mint, fresh foliage, dry leaves and the moist smell of greenery, the dirt of our dirt roads.

After dinner I went looking for the Bible again in the hopes of more reading. Gide took it away from me immediately. The harshness of his voice this afternoon was followed by a touching sweetness. This evening Gide is filled to the marrow with the peace of God. While he reads I study his face which has lost every trace of wear and tear. The oval is perfect, the features in repose. I recognize what he must have looked like as a young man, a face I was unable to find among his photographs when I wanted to compare it with the mask he now usually wears.

"Miraculous youthfulness! Perhaps God wills it thus . . ." my father told me later, half ironically, but all the same with just a serious enough tone to suggest that though he didn't dare state the fact as true he might at least allow it to pass under a simulated facetiousness. "God gives that, if nothing else, to the damned: they enjoy a worldly life particularly flourishing, protected, happy . . ."

133

This calculation which my father attributes to the deity reminded me of a remark of Pascal he quoted (and I must add that he was horrified) this very afternoon which contains a further example of this same inconceivable duplicity which they dare find in God: *We understand nothing of God's works if we take not as principle that He wishes to blind some and enlighten others . . . There is light enough to enlighten the Elect, and darkness enough for their humiliation. There is darkness enough to blind the reprobate and light enough for their condemnation . . .*

I have come to love that voice more and more as it swells and unfurls, overflowing, only to gather itself right away once more, and flow again. The first thing it sang was the story of Job. What a voice Gide gave Satan with "the sons of God" to accuse Job. But what tenderness he instilled into those words which the Eternal One addresses to Satan: "Behold, all that he hath is in thy power; only upon *himself* put not forth thine hand . . ." He chose the first few verses of Genesis next. His voice had such breadth that I felt myself transported far away, into a starry universe. Gide pointed out that there were *two* trees forbidden to Adam, the tree of life and the tree of the knowledge of good and evil. It was only the fruit of the latter which Adam and Eve got to.

"Oh, I know," said my father. "This is a rather ticklish passage. One sees God *afraid* of man here, suddenly afraid of being cast down by man . . ."

And Gide came to his assistance with, "And the LORD God said, 'Behold, the man is become as one of us, to know good and evil: and now lest he put forth his hand,

and take also of the tree of life, and eat, and live forever. Therefore the LORD God sent him forth from the garden of Eden . . .'"

"One is unable to understand, one dare not understand," I said. Gide called to our attention the magnificent passage, "And the eyes of them both were opened, and they knew that they were naked; and they sewed fig leaves together, and made themselves aprons. And they heard the voice of the LORD God walking in the garden in the cool of the day . . . ," and Gide cried, "That was the discovery of Conscience! Conscience which God had preferred not to have seen come into being . . . That was God threatened by man . . ."

My father added, pensively, "They are only images, of course . . . But the truth should hide beneath them. I would like to think so at any rate. Because whether the world is born of God or born of nothing the mystery remains the same. All in all the biblical hypothesis seems to me the more likely . . ."

Then one of those conversations took place which cannot help but sound trivial: Nonbeing, Infinity, Being. Then, without noticing it, we regained the earth and the measure of man. The art of Francis Jammes, so marvelous when he evokes the fields or the summer day, brought us back. Again Gide and my father recited admirable poems and once more I was able to compare those three voices that one man commands: the one so emphatic, dry, accented, of Gide reciting the poems he knows by heart (the ends of the phrases lengthen to end in a long, rustling sigh); another the more speedy delivery of his conversation, still more rhythmic than average, and finally the expert acrobatics of his reading voice

135

in which all the irregularities and accentuations of his other voices occur, but drowned in the grand lyric wave.

He was unable to go off to bed without reading us one more passage, the one in which the wisdom of Solomon is described.

Monday / July 3, 1939

Gide, seated in the hall, interrupts his reading of *En deçà de l'Honneur* to talk to me as I go by.

"That we should be so close in spite of our incredible difference of age astounds me . . . What friends we would have been if we were the same age, if we had only come to know each other when I was young . . ."

He goes on, his body turned, his face down. He points to various passages in my pamphlet that don't satisfy him. But on the whole he is pleased. We speak of our common anguish.

A.G.: Can you believe that anything else drove me to Communism? I felt a demand made upon me to *do something,* to try, to blast myself out of passivity. You have one advantage over me: you already recognize the falsity of your position. At your age I lived in luxury without knowing the inevitable injustice therein. Little by little, however, I grew to fear wealth. I gave up the majority of my rich friends. I visited poor people. That opened my eyes. But did I *do* anything?

C.M.: You have taken a *number* of chances . . . You

have dared be imprudent. You have *joined in*. The most recent example I find the most beautiful: your withdrawal from the Communist Party. You sacrificed your popularity when you saw that you could only enjoy it by sacrificing the truth.

My father entered the room. Interesting conversation between Gide and him.

A.G.: There is always this opposition between Catholicism and Christianity. As soon as I am close to a Catholic who appeals to me I realize that he is acting as a Christian, *against* the consensus of Catholic opinion. Thus Claudel represents Catholicism and you represent Christianity.

F.M.: Oh no, my dear friend, this is only an example of a struggle *within the Church,* between the spirit and the letter—and let me add right now that I am not so proud as to believe myself a representative of the spirit!

After a silence my father continued. "My religion brings certain consolations very precious to me: confession, first of all, that miraculous rejuvenation, with its certainty that no matter what we have done we can be pardoned, the joy at once again finding a clean page before us . . ."

"Which brings with it the added pleasure in blackening it!"

"Oh no, my dear Gide! You know of the ease of confession. But one ought not judge it by those who abuse it. You must admit that honest men do not confess without feeling true repentance. And besides there is no true confession without it. It is difficult, even unpleasant to go to confession . . ."

137

"You astound me! Why, it must be—what shall I say—it must be, yes, voluptuous!"

"You forget that not all sins are in the grand style. There are also our petty faults, ridiculous errors . . ."

"Yet that should be the same voluptuous pleasure as in humbling oneself!"

"As for me, I find it unpleasant. But what joy it brings! Then too my religion brings me a further consolation: communion. Thereby I have often avoided despair. After that what do I care about the mistakes, errors and injustices of the Church? I *judge* her according to what she is in this world, a worldly institution. You say that they very well might throw me out. If that ever happened I'd simply come in the other door. I will never give up Christ!"

"I hope they never do. If there were only more Catholics like you I'd join the Church myself . . ."

We walked through the field as far as the terrace. He named the plants and the insects. He looked young, calm, happy. Contradictions in this Proteus too sensitive to ever be One. One day he talks of the certainty for him of God's nonexistence, another day it's his desire to be a Christian—or of the possibility of conversion which implies the beginnings of faith.

Later my father remarked, "How vulnerable one feels he is. The longer we talk the more I feel he's persuaded. If we didn't know him better, you and I, wouldn't it be thinkable that he's very close to a conversion—after that conversation I mean. But a conversation with an enemy of Christ would have led him to similar agreement. I want to let him know for sure that I haven't the least desire to convert him. I prefer knowing that he's outside than inside because whether inside or out he won't be able to help stalking back and forth full of remorse near the door. All I can wish him is a deathbed conversion . . ."

4:00 P.M. My father's voice from the courtyard: "Claude!"

"What is it?"

"Gide left on foot for Langon and we're to pick him up there at 5:30. He wanted to be alone." Then suddenly, in a very ironic tone: "No doubt it was his intention to try a bit of hunting in the hills . . . He asked me if they don't swin in the Garonne. He intends to go stalking about down there . . ."

I laughed but without a good conscience. Nothing human seems laughable to me. The only value this journal has is the following: my testimony in good faith obeys the hypothesis that people must be taken seriously. A smile is permissible, of course, but not these belly laughs . . . I consider myself mercilessly every time I give in to the poor pleasure of a horse laugh.

In Langon.

A.G.: I took a walk along the Garonne. It was very *el*evating.

F.M. (ironically concerned): I bet there weren't many people . . .

A.G.: Oh a few, a few . . .

Magnificent night. At 10:00 "day wandered still at the foot of the sky." The moon rose to the chorus of crickets in a perfume from the meadows. Gide spoke of those two times he considered suicide. The first time was on his way to the army camp after induction, when he realized he would never live up to what was expected of him.

"In the train with my fellow-soldiers-to-be I was overcome by their vulgarity and obscenities. I really wanted to die. But that night, in the barracks, a corporal passed by the bed in which I pretended to be asleep. He looked at me and suddenly took up an overcoat and covered my legs. A joy flowed through me, and such happiness that I gave up the thought of suicide. The next morning I entered the infirmary because in spite of the solicitude of Corporal Herbette (that was his name) I'd caught cold. Two days after that I was discharged."

The second time was like this: after allowing himself to be carried away into making confessions to J.-É. Blanche, which covered him, Gide, with shame, he felt so nauseated, disgusted with himself and dirty that he wanted to die.

Our evening, in that gentle night, passed without incident. We played with a June bug dropped from heaven: Gide loves insects and in general everything that lives, with a respectful, attentive love.

Tuesday / July 4, 1939

News from Paris. My mother very disturbed by developments. "Thursday we were just about in despair." Rain. Lassitude. Will there be time for me to live? I made an appointment by telephone for Gide with a dentist in Bordeaux. After lunch the sun returned.

My father, barely whispering, because Gide went up for his nap in a room right over our heads: "I had a very serious conversation with him this morning. He came out with this astonishing sentence: 'If my wife could only know that I am here she would be very happy!' He started in again talking about the arts Catholics possess for entangling those outside. I answered with such thrust that he admitted I'd struck home. I was speaking about Julien Green. But he felt I could as well substitute Gide for Green. I said to him 'Forgive me, dear friend! There is no connection between a Jean Blanzat born in an anti-Christian home, or a Dabit brought up at the Hôtel du Nord, and a Green, for instance, a Green who knew Christ from his earliest days, and who gave him up for conscious reasons.' Gide shivered. I had touched a nerve . . . He is one of those creatures Péguy speaks of who are *permeable to grace.* Perhaps he is lost. But he is steeped in God. I've never met a person more spontaneously religious. I had to emphasize this point: there are conversions but no 'converters.' It's a relationship between God and yourself without a go-between. It will happen that at the right moment someone will be there to bear the name of priest, you'll see. But only as a means, not as a cause. He looked quite startled."

The same muffled voice continued: "One feels the corruption. But the evil hides itself with such art. How winning his ways are! What powers of seduction that immense intellect has in its catholicity and solidity! His stay will have been worthwhile, don't you think? At least *I* can't complain . . ."

141

We had dinner in Langon at Oliver's, outside under the scented linden. We spoke little, saving our attention for the conversation of our racy neighbors, students of pharmacy returned from an examination. Oliver's son intrigued Gide—and ourselves—with his simplicity. A positive Rasputin arrived, his face devoured by a black beard, a boater on his head and a young man behind him. They took a table at the other end of the garden. Gide, beside himself, couldn't keep still until we'd asked M. Oliver who he was, that apparition. But he didn't have the answer. All he knew was that he'd "never seen that much beard at the same time." Elated by a light dry wine we learned without sadness that the cinema, pretext for this trip to Langon, is closed Tuesdays. We got back to Malagar in good spirits and Gide began to read aloud at once: passages from the essay *l'Esprit de Conquête et l'Usurpation* by Benjamin Constant which Gide has a contemporary edition of. The euphoria that wine left me in prevents my understanding and often even listening. But even without really hearing them I know that these pages could have been written about Hitler, Stalin, Mussolini, with today's dateline.

My father has gone off to find *Atys,* the poem he has been working on for so many years—there are some selections from it in his most recent novel, *Les Chemins de la Mer.* He reads with a warm voice and his face lights up with all the nights, and all the fires of love. Gide says, half out loud, "It's altogether remarkable . . ." or, "Why, it's ex-tra-or-dinary!" or, "Totally *fine* . . ." And he sniffs, sighs and clears his throat. He pays such attention that at one point he interrupts to demand the restitution of a line. My father forgot to copy it into this manuscript. As for me, all I catch is the fire, naturally. Occasionally the beauties of this poem of carnal love sting me, but then only in sudden bursts. I intuit the grandeur of the work, but I do so really on the basis of little more than an infrequent scent. Once again I have reached my bounds. I find myself limited, a small desert island lost in the ocean, in an ocean whose wonders I will never know. Nothing can keep its secrets from me *up to a certain point.* But there my powers end. There I hit the switch marked OFF. And as I stand watching them, the more sensitive natures, the more intelligent, continue their progress alone. My momentum is broken at the point where theirs increases. The poem swells, overflows, and I find it lovely, moving—but I reproach myself with understanding no more and I envy Gide his ability to keep up. I have an inkling that in every domain of life I'm chained down in this way. My radius of action does not allow me long-distance flights. I can only accompany those high flyers a short distance . . . I think of that book I ought to write, the one about *in*-intelligence. Good title: *De l'Inintelligence.*

As for the intelligence of my inintelligence and the inintelligence of my intelligence I have already ex-plained myself sufficiently. This evening I think most of all about the dryness of my heart. My father's poem reminds me of an essential feature in his make-up that I am all too likely to overlook: he was once devoured by love. And then I look into my own poor heart, without mystery, almost without history . . . Perhaps my father used up all the love intended for several generations . . . I am all dried up. Every spring in me has run dry.

After *l'Atys païen* comes *l'Atys chrétien* and the

poem is done. Our guest allows his admiration to over-
flow. And it is no cliché in this case because that is literally
what Gide does.

A.G.: The published fragments of this poem excited
me but I thought that selection might have given them
their beauty. Now I see that the whole work is beautiful. Why don't you publish the poem? It would be a
surprise!

F.M.: Exactly . . . I'm too much afraid of a scandal.
This work contains such terrifying paganism that I've
destroyed it more than once. Each time I have found
enough old drafts to allow me to reconstruct it. Now I
no longer wish to destroy it . . .

A.G.: Finally! But why not publish?

F.M.: For so many young people, for so many people,
I represent something . . . I have such a responsible
position . . . And what's more, I realize that the position
is not *deserved*. What to do? Just the other day I
pleaded with the editors of *Temps Présent* to give me
my freedom. I have told them over and over that *I am
not worthy* of their pages, that I am hardly a "director
of conscience . . ." And they pleaded with me to go on . . .

A.G.: Of course your *Atys* is pagan, but won't you
gain in stature from it? And your position will seem
even more impressive: they will be able to see where
you began, what you built your faith on. And anyway,
the end of the poem is Christian, isn't it?

F.M.: The end? It isn't finished . . . My poem will
never be finished. I'll always be at work on it . . .

At this point I couldn't help interrupting. I did so
with growing enthusiasm and lyricism because I felt as

I spoke, thanks to Gide's agreement and the disquiet of my father, that I must be right. I told him that nothing seemed *purer* to me than this poem that had flowed from his deepest being. It was pure in the sense that it was *true,* born of the truth itself. With this wild flower, grown of its own accord from his body, I compared those infernal machines, dangerous, I believe, because they're so patiently constructed, and with what *care,* detail by detail—I mean his plays: the moment when M. Couture grasps the shoulders of little Emmanuele, when M. de Virelade torments Elisabeth about the accident with the revolver. Those reach the limits of what we can stand. Now I understand how my father could be disturbed about that—and it's there precisely that he does *not* think of his "responsibility." But the spontaneity and frankness of the *Atys* are incapable of doing harm: nature unfolds according to nature while *Asmodée* and *Les Mal-Aimés* use it as a pretext for clever, and harmful, variations . . .

Gide agrees and again advises publication—if absolutely necessary, under a pseudonym. My father seems rather upset: Gide and I have told him that what we believe to be dangerous in his plays can't be helped because it's their subject and it's all the beauty of their workmanship. He appears to be ready, thanks to our intervention, I'm certain, to *tone down* his *Mal-Aimés.* He doesn't seem to have realized that to do so would ruin the play. Neither Gide nor I are offended by the existence of a *Mal-Aimés.* On the contrary! But the existence of an *Atys* strikes us both as *a fortiori* worthy of our good offices.

Wednesday / July 5, 1939

Boring day in Bordeaux. Dinner with Gide and my father at the Guillemins. Errands in an overheated city —and it rained. Visit with Uncle Jean whom the presence of so important an unexpected guest put into a state where all he could do was stammer in a most affected style. Gide goes to the dentist. Gide offers his *Journal* to my father—who had just given me his own back at Malagar. Henri Guillemin, polite, but troubled —afraid Gide and my father are bored. He accompanies us until the minute of departure. At 6:00 we reach Malagar, all three of us considerably stupefied from our day in Bordeaux.

The late afternoon was gray and I took little pleasure in the readings my father chose from Verlaine. But soon enough the book was put aside, and memory sufficed, in fact had more power, in evoking the poetry in these poems and giving them life. In unison André Gide and François Mauriac recite, eyes almost closed, hands barely moving, voices clear:

> *Le ciel est, par-dessus le toit,*
> *Si bleu, si calme!*
> *Un arbre, par-dessus le toit,*
> *Berce sa palme . . .*

And then these lines, partly forgotten, but which they help each other recapture as their voices blend:

> *L'espoir luit comme un brin de paille dans l'étable . . .*
> *. . . Midi sonne. De grâce, éloignez-vous madame.*
> *Il dort. C'est étonnant comme les pas de femme*
> *Résonnent au cerveau des pauvres malheureux . . .*

146

And with the final *Ah! quand refleuriront les roses de septembre* their common emotion draws together.

Gide tells us, "I saw Verlaine three times. Once in the company of Pierre Louÿs, who reports our visit with precision in his *Vers et Prose*—and I've alluded to it near the beginning of my journal. He was in the Broussais hospital. And another time . . . So out of the ordinary that I'll never forget it: I was attracted by a mob of students at the gate of a *lycée* (Henri IV?). The youngest had surrounded a man and were jeering at him. It was Verlaine, drunk as a dog. He was wearing a top hat and since he'd lost his suspenders he held his trousers up with both hands. The children began to chase him. But he kept turning around as he stumbled away and shouted over and over *MERDE!* with a mixture of loathing and bravery. You'd have thought him an old boar set upon by curs."

"You came to his assistance?"

"Why no, what could I have done?"

And my father added something Paul Valéry told him: he used to run into Verlaine all the time but his condition was so pitiful that he was horrified—and turned away without saying a word.

Thursday / July 6, 1939

In his letters Jean Davray writes how curious he is about the journal I'm keeping. I am aware that I omit innumerable anecdotes which would give it charm in the eyes of my friend and my future readers. Today it was Montherlant, yesterday Jacques-Émile Blanche, other days Claudel, Copeau, Rivière or Proust—Gide and my father pile up their memories. By repeating them my journal would gain picturesqueness. But besides my difficulty in finding even the time to keep it up, such as it is, I have to admit being blind, almost, to the charms of the literary anecdote. Doubtless the reason for this is my being involved with these stories since my earliest years. The majority of the tales my father has entertained Gide with (and surprised him—Gide was unaware of my father's comic powers), I've known forever. I know them so well I'll probably never write them out. Too bad, I admit, especially that I've left out all Gide's stories. His visit has been much richer than my recital makes it. There has been, for instance, just the everyday life which has its interest. Gide's love of food, the charming way he has forced his routine on us, those too would be worth my attention. But my concern with the unique events of each day causes this neglect of what repeats itself each day: Gide's good morning, his good night, the way he sits at table with nonchalant elegance, his chair quite far from the table so he can cross his legs, and what he says about his night's sleep, his nap and his letters. And naturally I shall not go into the efforts of my father and myself to spare him any bother.

We spent the morning on the terrace in the sun. Gide and my father discussed the *Journal*—Gide's. Anecdotes began to pile up which again I've omitted. They mention that letter from Bergery (written on my advice, but Gide doesn't know that) which requests an article for the coming issue of *La Flèche* on the French Revolution. Once more our friend remarks on his inability of writing anything for the time being. "One thing that ought to reassure you," my father tells him, "is your *Journal*: all your life you've been obsessed by that feeling. Because you are Gide, no other reason, and between you and your work intervenes your critical spirit, your intellect and your consuming love of life."

Gide recalled then that he had been so discouraged by the reviews of *l'Immoraliste* that he went seven years without writing a thing—until *La Porte Etroite*. He spoke of the failure each of his early works suffered at its publication. He congratulates himself for this preliminary lack of success. Success would have changed him. He would have been deprived of that distance which is his total *raison d'être*. He admits that if he had been a theatrical success he would have gone on writing plays, nothing else, and even made concessions to the taste of his public.

My father would like to believe that there isn't a single encounter which is not willed by a hidden power— God, I guess. Perhaps the beginning of the friendship which Gide feels for me had no other reason than to bring him nearer François Mauriac—but neither of us could have even guessed that. So I shall not have acted as anything but a go-between. But last night he took advantage of a short absence of my father to whisper, "I would not have dared show to François Mauriac what I let you read in Paris . . ."

Sincerely surprised—and I wouldn't have been a week

149

ago—I answered, "Better than I can, he would understand it all . . ." That Gide should allude to a special confidence he made me is a shock. I had already made up my mind that I'd disappointed him. Yes, I'd made up my mind, and the brief attempts Gide had made on my sentiments, although they proved to me that he did not find me totally unappetizing, were unable to restore any of my past illusions. This visit will have one result: Gide will discover all my limits and I will at least guess his and that ought to make his friendship seem less desirable. I mean that his company and the reading of his *Journal* have taught me that he plans everything in advance, even his weaknesses. The spontaneity that touched me so in Paris I now recognize as something he stands in control of—with a more or less conscious perfidy. We lied to one another again more or less willfully, because we both of us wished to please ourselves.

My father shines and I am silent. I find a place for myself in the shade. I stay in it without jealousy. It happens, as I said, that Gide seeks me out in my refuge. Once more he takes me into his confidence, his affection. I feel embarrassment and do nothing to encourage him. Thus I allowed his attempted conversation of yesterday to get by. I must have seemed cautious and self-absorbed. He had his hands on nothing more than a clam which plays dead. I must say this of myself, though to do myself justice, not once during Gide's stay have I tried to exceed myself just to excite his esteem. Continuously I have been myself, natural, and never made the least effort to seem less prosaic, insignificant and banal than I am.

Gide took me at my word. Today I saw in my father's

hands that little brick-red copybook: his conjugal adventure.

After dinner my father reads his short essay on Pascal written for publication in America. Gide repeats "How dreadful!" like a *leitmotif* at every mention of Jansenism. In this state of exhaustion I enjoy nothing and least of all listening to Gide.

Friday / July 7, 1939

Listen to Gide, put questions to him, I haven't the strength. Some sort of disgust overwhelms me that only the decision to make something printable out of *En deçà de l'Honneur* dispels for a moment. Cocteau can wait. Not this testimony. Once more, just as last September, the possibility of death spurs me on. It's high time to make one's testament.

Morning spent reading Gide's *Journal* in the courtyard next to Gide himself, who reads my father's *Mystère Frontenac*. No communication between us. After having made up his mind to write the article Bergery wants, he gives up for lack of ideas and out of laziness: "I wish they'd leave me alone . . . I don't know what I think of the Revolution any more . . . Don't I deserve at last that they should leave me alone?" I understand his discouragement and that he demands tranquillity. But I am obligated morally in Bergery's eyes. And I am rather annoyed with myself for having overestimated my credit with Gide.

My father and I discuss these famous conjugal notes.

CONVERSATIONS WITH ANDRÉ GIDE

C.M.: Aren't you astonished too at the power which forces him to write *and to reveal* such confessions? He was as unable to keep from you as from me these—his most painful secrets . . .

F.M.: It's part of his personality. I'd almost say his sickness. When he asked me whether I thought he could publish this *Journal* I thought, "You know perfectly well you're going to publish, that you can't do anything else, so why pretend you want to know what I think?"

C.M.: That business in the train—frightful, isn't it?

F.M.: Frightful! Right there we catch the amount of involuntary action, of the unavoidable in Gide's case. In front of his wife, on their honeymoon . . . Not even an attempt to hide from her what was going on . . . Inconceivable! I asked him squarely how he could allow himself—and got this humble answer, "I could not act otherwise. It was stronger than I. There was nothing to be done. Nothing, do you understand, absolutely nothing was going to stand in the way of my . . ." I also remarked to him that his wife would hardly have been consoled by reading these notes. Don't we see him crying about himself and not about her when she burns all his letters? And he answered I was right and that possibly his wife destroyed them because they were written more to posterity than to herself, or at any rate to posterity *as much* as her. "What I find so wonderful about you," I told him, "is that *in spite of everything* you have held on to your marvelous delicacy . . ."

Seeing him walk off just now, my father praised his kindness, intelligence and *grandeur*. He admits that Gide's visit has brought them closer and that he's deeply fond of Gide. Part of Gide's mystery, this reconciling of irreconcilables. No question but my father is much more troubled than I by the "impurities" of Gide's life. But he respects him, is as fond of him as I am.

Not a day passes that my father doesn't make some mention of the thousand and one obstacles that prevent his expressing himself frankly on this or that subject: his responsibility as a Catholic writer, filial piety and so on . . . That Gide doesn't deplore at the top of his lungs this timidity or delicacy . . . Yesterday he burst out, "But you, you are covered with chains!" And today after reading extracts from Pascal's *xvie Provinciale* (*"Vous me faites pitié, mes Pères!"*) my father regretted not being able to write the good pamphlets that the hour calls for and gave as his reason, "No one would be interested. . ." Gide burst out with a horse laugh. His voice became pressing, tempting: "Go ahead! Go ahead, dear friend, don't hesitate! No readers! That's too funny . . ."

Towards the end of the afternoon Gide and I revisited the settlement of refugees at Verdelais where the two charming households received us. My father had sent them two autographed books by me, and Gide, who is usually so stingy with his signature (the copy of the *Journal* he gave my father he only signed after repeatedly remarking with boorish insistence how rare signed copies of his works are), Gide felt he neither should nor could refuse these banished Spaniards: he brought back the two volumes they brought the other day for him to inscribe. As soon as we got there Gide dragged me into a barn where children were playing blindman's buff. But our ill-timed intrusion disturbed them. They broke off their game to surround us with their sweaty faces upturned in laughter. Gide said he was sorry he never

153

learned Spanish . . . One of our refugee friends arrived
and took us into the little office where we were several
days ago. The two young women, their husbands, Gide
and I, all of us felt a new confidence that put us at ease.
No longer sudden embarrassments on either side. They
told us the story of their flight, of friends shot right at
the border and even by other Nationalists who had
caught up with them, of the days in the snow, without
food and over the clogged roads of France—and further
back in the past, the bombing of Lerida during which
one of the young women had lost her mother, their
hasty marriages . . . They told us how disappointed they
were yesterday in Bordeaux to learn that the boats to
Santo Domingo are full and they won't be able to leave
before September.

A momentary disturbance brought us outside. It was
short and pathetic. Every woman and child in the settlement surrounded an old trap in which two girls and a
boy sat somehow in a mass of formless packages. Their
families had obtained the authorization for them to return to Spain . . . The boy's face seemed lit up with joy
and at the same time full of an emotion very like pain.
He was hugging our friends the nurses—they had taken
turns for some time at the head of his bed after he took
sick in the snows of Puygcerda. One of them cried.
Among those who remained there were many tearful
faces. Hands held out. That little crowd in multicolor
rags milled around and the racket it made put us down
in another world, very far from France. Gide got closer.
I shook the boy's hand. I too raised an arm in good-bye
as though they had been my friends. It occurred to me
that these people who have known so many sorrows to-

gether and perhaps as many joys will very probably never see each other again. The boy hugs a young girl. They tell each other, *"Au revoir!"* as though they will meet again soon . . .

And the wagon goes off into the dust accompanied by the shouts of children. Tomorrow they will be in Spain because someone there wants to have them. And the terror still reigns in Spain. (My father heard this morning that every day they shoot one hundred Basques . . .) Spain, which the majority of these refugees will never see again . . .

This all lasted about one minute . . .

Gide and I went back into the little office, both moved still by this departure, sad, beautiful, in which we had taken part. Gide took our friends' names and addresses. It seemed to me that he had grown so fond of them that the idea of leaving them forever was insupportable. He dawdled. He could only tear himself away after promising to come back again before his departure.

Magnificent evening which allowed us to enjoy its coolness. Gide and I set fire to a bit of flowers of sulphur which the duster lost near the vines: the experiment fascinates us as much as it bores my father—the childish interest we have in the bubbling of the sulphuric and the release of the sulphurous acid are lost on him. He paws the ground like a tethered horse. We follow after him down the alley of young cypress. Because of his height my father pokes above the skyline: his profile defines itself against the sky. Gide, somewhat shorter, cuts a darker silhouette against the landscape where the mists of evening spread. He is reciting Vigny and my father accompanies him:

> *Aimons ce que jamais on ne verra deux fois . . .*

He recites some Rimbaud and for once my memory is good and I can mix my voice with theirs:

> *Mais vrai j'ai trop pleuré, les aubes sont navrantes,*
> *L'âcre amour m'a gonflé de torpeurs enivrantes . . .*

Then, home again, my father reads bits of Péguy. I am a little disappointed: his *Note Conjointe* used to knock me out . . . I can not recover the former emotion Next Gide reads one of the stories in *Scènes de la Vie Parisienne: Profil de marquise.* "I don't like it at all when Balzac tries to be graceful," my father says. "Then his chatter sounds so heavy!" It was lovely all the same. Gide acted it all out; he read with infinite wit; he added all his own lightness to something which might very well have been a trifle heavy. And then we had spoken of Balzac so much today and of all the pleasures we owed him, all three of us, that it was a good idea for us to hear him read aloud, even if the passage chosen were relatively bad.

Saturday / July 8, 1939

Gide had me type out in triplicate a letter to a Belgian paper which ran a criticism of the *Montaigne* which appeared under his name: he disavows it almost completely.

Morning, lunch, coffee: ease, simplicity in our relations. The silences are numerous but the cause of no embarrassment. Our conversation is easy, restful, without pretensions, pleasing.

6:00 P.M. At my window, "Gide's gone?"

My father in the courtyard: "Yes, I walked with him as far as the terrace. We saw two snakes there, one tremendous. Gide was enchanted! Then he hurried off down the road like an old faun . . ."

We both felt that we ought not to go with him. A number of *La Révolution Prolétarienne* which contained a report of the end of the fighting in Spain served as his pretext—he wanted to have it translated for his Spanish friends. It's clear that the settlement of refugees attracts him. The other day he left alone for Verdelais—but was unable to find the road. I strongly suspect him of being interested in those laughing dark boys who play pelota in the dust of the road in front of the gate . . .

My father to Gide: "Your *Journal* as far as I've gotten depresses me so . . . Those years you spent seeing so many interesting people, 1910–1912, I too spent in Paris, and doing what? True that I had no reason for running into your great friends of those days . . . But what luck Claude has had! What a youth he has . . ." And turning to me: "In this exciting life of yours, the most interesting men of your time, you may find a sterilizing virus . . ."

And Gide agreed. My father continues that without a doubt it was the youth that he had that enabled him to become a creator . . . And I am haunted by the word "sterilizing" that he just threw in without attaching any importance to it—but it hurts.

Meanwhile Gide had vanished.

157

"What saved him, and his *Journal* supports this," my father said to me, "is the tremendous appetite he has for every kind of work, and which has made such a cultivated gentleman of him. Literature, music, languages, and with what application he has pursued it all, with method and bravery so that a sort of moral rectitude and strength has guided his way of living. He has escaped from every downfall that's menaced him, thanks to this marvelous taste for study and learning and perfection . . ."

He continued: "I'm struck too by his overpowering lack of conscience, his naïveté: not once has he truly realized what he might have been for his wife, his parents—or poor Drouin of whom he speaks with such an incomprehensible ignorance! He has come to be convinced that his case, when all is said and done, has very little importance. The full measure of embarrassment and pain that he caused his family never got through to him completely . . ."

Gide returned radiant from his long walk. It seemed to have awakened a sort of well-being in him—at least that's how I interpreted it . . . After dinner my father read aloud from Claudel's *La Messe Là-bas*. Together, he and Gide sang Claudel's praises . . .

Before going to bed, Gide takes a turn in the garden. He appears in the window. Against the night every feature, every gesture obtains a certain relief. I seem to be seeing him for the first time and feel again astonishment that he is here. With graceful negligence he props himself on his elbows: the face is again that young face of so many years ago. The nonchalance of his stance, the elegance, the harmony in carelessness, belong to another age. I watch him with all my attention—before it's too late. I hadn't seen so much of him over the last few days—the first week here our schedule brought us together more often—and I had almost forgotten he is here, and what he means. Happily! I might add. Nothing was so exhausting as the continual attentiveness of those first few days . . . And now once more he appears with his legendary features and in that languid pose which will always be his. There he is, smiling, young, present as he was in my memory of a previous evening.

This scene lasted half a minute. He went up to bed. "How sad he is this evening," my father whispered. "He suffers from remorse, I'm certain . . . Face to face with death he considers what he's been. Certainly, he feels remorse . . . Growing old is hard . . ." And I think: Not remorse, *regrets!* Certainly, he is face to face with an approaching nothingness. Here we are surrounding him with affection and attentions but there is also a part of his being for which we can do nothing and which feels death's approach. I picture him all of a sudden. He is lying in bed. He thinks of our kindness but recognizes the deeper indifference it covers. I'm disturbed about his health in the morning but I won't cry when I hear he's dead. He is alone. And who really loves him? Who really holds his love, however little, between his death and him? He hears the shutters being closed. Does he know that before I closed those shutters and went to bed I sat here with my elbows on the window sill? The night belongs to stars and wind. A light wind that makes the foliage rustle gently, a wind laden with every odor on earth and all heaven's solitude . . . That forbidden world where it would be possible to join in the games of night, where every envious look and all waiting would have an end, tears my mind apart. The tears I imagined in Gide's eyes almost pour from my own. It is no longer a question of his age or my age; I know there is no "age" against eternity.

Sunday / July 9, 1939

Gide calls me to his room. After having read me a letter from our friend André Dubois, he lets me in on a scheme of his, a demonic scheme: make Claudel aid in the funds being raised for the Spanish intellectuals in exile in France—against his will! He intends to do so by selling a manuscript that Claudel gave him that is now worth 20,000 francs. He reads me the beginning of an article he's just finished: "I'm rubbing my hands. I've just played a fine trick on Paul Claudel . . ."

My father walks in. Gide starts reading all over again and with the same happy tone. "Good for the sale of that manuscript! But the article? I don't know . . . You take the responsibility—if you can . . ." When we were alone my father said, "He really does lack conscience: think of trying to teach Claudel a lesson like that!"

Mass at Verdelais, 10:30 A.M., with my father. He

160

congratulates himself for not bringing Gide as he had at first believed he should—and Gide said later that he had almost asked if he could come. "The devil had everything ready for you," my father laughed. "Two sermons of abject stupidity, Massenet's *Claire de lune* during the consecration. Everything that would disgust you most. I was in despair! Lord, what they are able to *do* to that miracle the mass!"

It's obvious that my father is trying to keep separate in the mind of Gide the faith on the one hand and what men do on the other. He refuses to make any confusion between Christ and what human weakness or cowardice commit in His name.

Uncle Jean for lunch. Much more natural this time, in fact very natural. Gide must see by now how little bigotry there is in the Mauriac family. Our broad-mindedness, or rather that of my uncle the l'Abbé, and my father's, must be an agreeable surprise. Interesting conversation about Franco Spain, *l'Action Française,* the OGPU and so forth . . . Gide tells us how he dined with Rivet at Léon Blum's while Blum was Premier and then that very night had their conversation repeated to him by his friend Pierre Herbart, who was still a member of the Communist Party, word for word, and since then he'd found other reasons to be certain—and had indeed recently spoken with Blum, who agreed with him—that the Communists must have a microphone concealed in the fireplace and there was nothing the Premier said that the Communists didn't know, immediately. That reminded me of something Davray told me the other day, he'd heard it from a relative of Blum:

Blum was so carefully guarded by his backers when he was in power that his own brother was unable to reach him. He saw the Premier making gross errors, wanted to warn him, to shout, "Watch out!" But there were innumerable obstacles placed between his brother and him. One day, long after this, he succeeded in having lunch with Léon Blum and telling him some facts that were particularly serious. Blum cried, stupefied, "Are you absolutely sure of the truth of that?" And his brother laughed bitterly, "*You* were Premier . . . You were also the only person in France who didn't know this!"

And that is what power is.

And I remembered another picture of Blum André Dubois painted me the other day. At that time Dubois was *sous-préfet* in an industrial town in the north that had been racked for a long time by strikes. He described Blum, completely wild, at the end of his tether, whining, "These factory owners are heartless. What do they expect me to do? Am I supposed to throw myself at their feet? I would do that too if it were any use. I would do *anything* . . . What though? Are they really monsters? Don't they have hearts at all?"

And Dubois also told me how Salengro, then Minister of the Interior, locked himself in Dubois' office after making clear that no one should bother them; standing before Dubois, very pale and stammering, "Man to man, Dubois, do you believe that I've deserted the cause the way *Gringoire* has accused me of doing?" That was several days before his suicide. And that is what power is . . .

Uncle Raymond and Uncle Pierre come for tea as arranged. The Brothers Karamazov reunited around

Gide . . . On the subject of the Claudel-Maritain business, about Guillemin's article too, Gide and my father and I scandalize our guests and especially Uncle Pierre, whose beautiful face, first so animated with ironic attention, goes dark. He had obviously decided not to give in to his political passions, therefore he was able to dismiss ours, under control as we kept them, with an indulgent smile. But we could feel from time to time he was on the point of shouting, he was so scandalized. We touched, with some sadism, I admit, on the most delicate topics, but were careful not to go too far, *i.e.,* we spoke of Franco but never mentioned *l'Action Française.* Everyone took part, and our conversation thus reached an agreeable insignificance . . . The reunion of the Mauriac brothers for Gide, the presence of Gide for the Mauriac brothers—those were attractions enough!

After my uncles left we three went to Saint-Macaire. The light that fills Giorgione's paintings transfigured the tawny stone along ancient streets; the romanesque church; the valley of the Garonne as it's seen from the high ramparts from under the shiver of willows; an outdoor dance we visited at the foot of the walls . . . There we watched the frenetic high spirits of dancers, young people from Bordeaux in buses. This was (a banner let us in on it) a festival given by an association of small businessmen of Saint-Macaire. Along the walls and on top of a tower boys were chasing each other with wild gestures; the orchestra struggled to do its best and the girls jumped happily, red with enjoyment, heat—in the arms of boastful boys with singing accents . . . Gide seemed to move easily through the fair—my father too.

We were conscious most of all of that light which gilds, and of the world's peaceful children . . . The calm Garonne flowing between its calm banks formed a great arch fogged over with sun. "To be a painter . . ." said my father, "and make that miracle hold still . . ." The crowd spreading out carried its joy among the willows. Even the buses and their jocular drivers adding noise were unable to make them shy . . .

After dinner I read aloud from my journal.

Monday / July 10, 1939

Gide writes in front of me: the text of a telegram announcing to Mme. de Lestrange our imminent arrival in Chitré. After much hesitation my father and I ended by accepting this invitation. I'm happy because it means Gide will be among us longer. I'm so awfully attached to him—in spite of what I may think, say and write on this subject—that the idea of his leaving tortures me . . .

André Gide speaks with such understanding and emotion of my last night's reading that I lead him to my room and read him my journal from Mézière so that he will have a better idea of the Abbé Jacques Laval than he could have had yesterday evening. I read him those terrible days, September 25 and 26, 1938. When I closed the notebook he was in tears! All he could do was place a hand on my shoulder—and run. The bell rang for lunch a few minutes after this and he appeared with a new face.

I was touched by the attention and interest he gave that reading. There he sat in the big chair with the yellow slip cover in front of the little table . . . Muffled syllables of approbation, or emotion, punctuated my reading. I revealed to him certain very intimate sides of my life and he cried. Can I ever forget that?

I said to him, "We have only begun to really talk now that we must part . . ."

And he answered, "We will never part, Claude, now I know for sure . . ."

Then he mentioned a possible visit I might pay him at Cuverville. He congratulated me (and with a somewhat conspiratorial sympathy) when I told him, "Nothing seems stranger to me than material ambition . . . Work yourself to death, give up every possibility of self-improvement, and more than that, every direct and living contact with reality, just to guarantee a pension at age sixty! Life is too short for the honors and rewards heaped up in it to seem anything but small to me. Not that I lack ambition. But my ambition aims higher than a position as ambassador or a professorship of laws . . ."

And he agreed, and not without warmth: "I am praised from time to time for renouncing this or that advantage. The truth is I didn't want it. Not at any price! I simply don't need it . . ." He was struck in particular by what he learned about Abbé Jacques Laval from my journal and the remarks I made.

"How old is he?"

"Twenty-seven, I believe . . ."

"Twenty-seven!" It was a cry of pain. Twenty-seven and renounce life like that. Give up, at twenty-seven, so much that at seventy still charms . . .

I said, "Even if Jacques Laval is mistaken, even if that God doesn't exist, he will not have suffered in vain. A life that full of love and sacrifice accompanied with so much beauty cannot help but increase our human stature . . ." Gide didn't deny it. He whispered, "Now I understand you better, Claude. I have found the dramas among which your life moves. Yes, I understand better now . . ."

No difference of age or of importance exists for us now. We are two friends or two brothers. Our conversation was not bogged down in the least embarrassment. Beyond good manners and literature we allowed our hearts to open . . .

After lunch I typed a letter for Gide, concerning a German refugee, wrote my journal and then typed out three articles and a letter for my father.

Gide wears himself out trying to close his suitcase: the locks have been forced. I watch him with surprise. He grumbles without let-up, "This is grotesque!" He squats there making useless efforts. The veins in his pink scalp swell. That André Gide could *also* be an old gentleman losing his temper over a ruined suitcase, in my naïveté such an idea had never occurred to me . . .

Late in the afternoon he came timidly to ask me politely (his sweet smile) for another reading. I read him, day by day, the end of August and beginning of September of last year. It isn't exciting, but all the same he seemed visibly excited. The bell announcing dinner interrupts us and we both regretted having to stop . . .

Evening: selections from Corneille's *Pompée* read by my father and a bit of *Psyché* by Gide. After Gide had left for bed my father said, "I've just finished reading his *Journal,* 1917. He's dying of love for Michel. What cries—and how often marvelous! And what courage in publishing . . . He is one man who, by nature, cannot stand falsehood. It's necessary for him to hide nothing. This demand on his part I'll have to admit gives him a miraculous virginity and purity . . ."

PART THREE

Chitré

Tuesday / July 11, 1939

Left Malagar at 9:00 A.M. I'm at the wheel, Gide beside me and Father in back. Stop at Blasimon, where we were attracted by the flowers strewn at a wedding which unfortunately we were unable to locate. So I have seen Gide a second time in front of the ancient Abbey, under trees in a mystery they cast somewhat as those do at Olympia. Another stop, Castillon, where we visited the lovely church, 17th century. The landscape has charm. Gide proclaims himself enchanted and tells us nothing pleases him more than a trip like this.

Montaigne . . . I had counted on a great deal from such a pilgrimage in the company of Gide and my father. And indeed we did put piety into our visit to the tower. And we stayed a long time in *"la librairie,"* attentive, discreet, full of silent fervor. I watched Gide: he was spelling out the Latin quotations engraved on the ancient beams; he went over a passage Montaigne had written about La Boétie—and my father muses . . . In their minds—as in mine—the same disappointment. Montaigne inhabits my heart; I look into my heart and there is his tower. He's warm there. I smell the comfort and the presences warm and heavy as any house that is lived in has them. Here in the places where he once lived I find no trace. These abandoned rooms, their cracking walls covered with stupid graffiti (not even contact with Montaigne can separate tourists from their grossness), are deader than dead. These tiles bore the weight of Montaigne but knew no way to hold him. The small courtyard below is just as he left it; behind the horror of a recently rebuilt château the old terrace and the enormous view of woods were as they ought to be . . . Nothing whatsoever happened inside me, not a drop of emotion. Only this one thing amuses me: to be with Gide in this place he has never been to, here where my father laughingly says he finds his very Lourdes.

We were on the road the rest of the morning: after Périgueux we stopped in Brantôme for lunch. Another famous site, but all we had time to appreciate was its best restaurant. We sat on the terrace of the old Hotel Chabrol and enjoyed *pâté de fois gras, pâté de lièvre,* omelets with truffles, chicken and mushrooms. The hostess discovered my father; carried away by pride and carrying on with tireless obstinacy and woeful taste, she lists those celebrities, who—"just like François Mauriac" —have entered her restaurant. She brings out her autograph books ("autocrats" she calls them) and burbles out the famous names from Sarah Bernhardt to Marshal Pétain. Gide doesn't say a word. Finally my father draws the attention of our talkative hostess to another famous man who honors her table, otherwise famous than himself and otherwise glorious, in fact, almost as much though he may not act it (and I say almost, but just a little less!) than Pétain himself: in short, that's André Gide.

Who? Gide. André Gide.

"Monsieur also writes perhaps?"

"Yes," answers Gide with a humble smile.

"Would you be so kind as to tell me in what magazine?"

"In *la Flèche*," says Gide as serious as he can be.

"Gyps, did you say? Yes, I seem to have seen that name there."

Since she was terribly pretentious, she galloped back several times in the hope of making good the bad impression her ignorance had caused, and trying, if possible, to learn a little too. André Gide answered her each time with the same smiling affability. And my father paraphrased the Gospels to the effect, "Woe to her who did not know when she was visited . . ."

The whole afternoon behind the wheel with Gide silent next to me but not the least bit sleepy, and even attentive to the smallest details that made our drive picturesque. Angoulême, Poitiers, and soon after Vouneil-sur-Vienne, and down there the imposing white mass of the château of Chitré. The Vicomtesse de Lestrange greeted us warmly. She lives alone here with her young son, Michel, and his teacher, Miss Adams. Enormous rooms, profusion of stag heads, stuffed birds, massive furniture, bibelots. The landscape surrounding us is rich but sad, and seen from a great distance since the high main building is protected from the country and is even separated from the park by an important moat. The windows set too high to allow a good view of the gardens.

Everything here seems to have been designed to add to the melancholy. For dinner our tiny table was arranged in the corner of a tremendous hall—the butler came out a door at the other end, very tiny. Silences cut off our attempts at conversation. I recalled Gide's energy. He has not yet found it here: every sentence he came out with was trivial. Now it was his turn, as it had been ours the first few days at Malagar, to worry about whether we were enjoying ourselves.

Before I retired to the great waiting room of a bedroom I had been assigned, I accompanied Gide to his: his canopied bed, the beamed ceiling! Why here was the real room of Montaigne, totally different from the one we saw this morning! We laughed like children, about nothing, about everything.

Chitré, Wednesday / July 12, 1939

A dog barking at the moon prevented my father sleeping. "What solitude," he says. "How does Gide stand it? Not even one little shepherd boy on the horizon . . ."

Lunch in the country restaurant at Vouneil. (Most of Mme. de Lestrange's servants are away.) Day spent working on the car: just a wheel to change but there were complications. Ride afterwards to a romanesque church in the neighborhood, Chauvigny. Gide and I admired the capitals. Back in Chitré he asked me to read him the rest of my journal for September 1938. (Yesterday morning he insisted I bring several notebooks with me to supply us with worthwhile reading . . .) For a moment he is again close to tears. But I am embarrassed by the monotony of my reading. How many weaknesses the pages reveal! A bit worried too by what Gide *really* thinks of all this, leaving out of account his emotional nature, the manifestations of which say nothing one way or the other about the *value* of my testimony.

After dinner Gide and Mme. de Lestrange play out a game of chess. Then Gide and my father alternate in reading aloud from Mme. de Sévigné's letters. How painfully this evocation of a dead society touches me . . .

Thursday / July 13, 1939

I had hardly finished shaving when Gide timidly asked if he could presume on my hospitality. When he talks of my journal Gide speaks with difficulty, as at his freest moments, in an embarrassed way, hesitant, covering the emotion. "I understand the place in your life which a being like your friend the Abbé Laval holds. He deserves it. But I can't help asking myself this agonizing question: Is it impossible to attain to any grandeur without committing a fraud against reason?"

"But for Abbé Laval," I cried, "faith is a matter of fact and his reason finds as complete satisfaction as his heart. And if he is mistaken and his faith has no foundation in an absolute sense, then the beauty of his life is still real . . ."

"That's exactly where my trouble lies. Is there to be

175

no beauty and dignity *without* that deceit? Because as
you know, Claude, I'm *no longer* troubled, really. I'm
as sure as I am of anything that there's nothing more self-
contradictory than the ideas we have of God, that God
doesn't exist, nor 'eternity.' "

"That may very well be, I'm sorry to say! And even
more serious: I see nothing whatsoever that renders me
worthy of eternity. I simply don't deserve it . . ."

"Better still," Gide interrupted, "I don't feel any
need for it. The older I get the better the idea of death
strikes me. I am less and less demanding. I no longer
fight back . . . No, the whole Christian conception is
absurd. Absurd . . . I cannot accept it and the idea of
reward revolts me as much as that of eternity. 'Eternal
life' corresponds to nothing within me. I can see our
earthly life with its parade of miseries about which
something must be done. And if I do a good deed it is
not out of a desire for rewards, but because I feel the
need to do them. And then I think of your friend Laval,
whom I cannot help admiring, of course. And I ask myself sadly: Is it impossible for a man to attain this grandeur without subterfuge? Oh, I know for a Laval there is
no subterfuge—but *I* know that he's fooling himself."

"What do you know about it really? And if he and
not you should be right, it is upon you (and myself too,
alas!) that the word *blind* will stick. According to that
hypothesis it is Grace which both you and I lack."

"I don't understand that. *Everything* in me pulls back
from faith. I am told that it is out of pride. What poverty! What could mere pride do between a God and
man? I am not so silly all the same, nor so presumptu-
ous. Why can't they comprehend that I am an unbe-

176

liever out of *honesty?* Nor can I prevent myself from deploring that it is by means of an illusion that the best people find it necessary to become greater. Is there really no human dignity possible outside the Christian religion with all its self-denial and inhuman sacrifice? I keep coming back to it because it's so close to my heart . . . Why is it necessary for a Laval to sacrifice the flesh, to humble it?"

"Perhaps because one must be strong, physically strong, and in another sense morally, too, to choose evil, to abandon onself without forfeit to one's instincts . . ."

He didn't answer but I could tell he was thinking, "Exactly, there are also the strong . . ." This silence lasted a little, then I said, "The whole of Antiquity testifies in favor of your conception of a human greatness compatible with Reason. Of a peace which the notion of Nonbeing cannot reach. Of serene acceptance of despair . . ." But I was thinking, "The same thoughts trouble him that trouble me . . . Can it be possible that at seventy, at the end of a life of study, meditation and enriching experiences, I too will come to this? From twenty to seventy, not a step forward . . . Is that possible?"

The remainder of the morning we devoted to more of my journal: Trip through Czechoslovakia. I can not disentangle the motives Gide has for listening to all this. Can he find human interest? literary interest? That would be fine. But I'm afraid that curiosity alone leads him to discover exactly who I am, who my friends are, and what face I present to the world. Able to see nothing more than the weaknesses of this journal and its thousands of little accommodations, I feel an increasing

177

embarrassment at Gide's interest. Gide said one thing, though, which surprised me a good deal: "Something more than mere laziness has always prevented me from regularly writing up a journal: often I have experienced a need to forget myself. To keep one's eyes on oneself continually as you do is *dangerous, it dries one up* . . ."

We spent the end of the day in Poitiers where Gide dragged me all over town looking up his old friend Jehl—who wasn't home. Then returned to Mme. de Lestrange and my father and visited the best churches: Sainte-Radegonde and of course Saint-Hilaire . . . Gide was afraid of catching cold and barely stepped inside those cool vaults before taking off!

Back at Chitré Gide again asks me to read to him. Tired of reading my own journal I take up Jacques Laval's, or rather the selections that he sent me just before we left Malagar the other day. I chose those cries of fatigue, despair and joy from his twenty-sixth year. I did my best and Gide listened with fervor. All these confidential diaries—it's almost funny, but Gide never smiled. Repeating his whispers of this morning: "I understand the place Laval has in your life . . . I understand better and better . . ."

"There's no literature in *this* journal . . ."

"Nor in yours either, Claude . . . These two testimonies illuminate each other . . ."

"My life is so poor next to his! I have never before read as in these last few days so much of my journal consecutively. What strikes me most is the monotony and it results from the monotony of my life. What I need is an *encounter*. I must encounter someone as noble and courageous as Jacques but who can lead me along paths I can follow. A dangerous path, naturally, and one that will enrich me, but one cut out for *me*. I could not follow Jacques—his God was never mine. I need some sort of Rimbaud. I'd follow him to the end of the world. If you know such a Master, arrange this encounter: I need him! I'm suffocating, you know. There is still time, but there is just time enough to save me from sinking in the drowsy comforts of the bourgeoisie. Alone I wouldn't have courage to escape. What stops me most of all is this complete absence of imagination which my cowardice and laziness make the most of. What to do, where to turn? I need ideas! If only a being would appear whom I might love, admire, I'd be saved . . ."

It was getting late. We had to hurry off and change for dinner—the easy charm of Malagar was not in order here. Gide, obviously touched, took both my hands in his and squeezed them. And I ran off.

After chess that evening Gide read us a short tale of Voltaire's, chosen because it testified in favor of our conversation about faith of this morning, its impossibility: *Le Bon Bramin.* Next he took a volume of Saint-Exupéry (who is a cousin of Mme. de Lestrange), *Terre des Hommes,* and read us a fine passage I already knew: Guillaumet, crashed in the Andes, conquers cold, hunger and despair to save his life—with what effort: "What I accomplished there no animal, I can assure you, could have accomplished."

179

Between Gide and myself, today, and perhaps for the first time really, not an atom of literature has intervened. He is no longer a celebrity. I am no longer a young man. We were *two men,* that's all, two men who understood each other . . .

Strange, reading fifty years of the journal when all day long its author is right there . . . My father and I never stop reading Gide except to talk to Gide.

Friday / July 14, 1939

This morning I had hardly finished writing up the events of yesterday when Gide knocked timidly. "I'm returning your friend's journal. Last night I read it from cover to cover. With some interest, you can imagine—and with emotion." He sat down in a large armchair with the light behind him. "What you said last night about the necessity you stand in of finding a Master startled me. I'm sure it is very bad for you to entertain such doubts of yourself . . ."

C.M.: I know myself, be sure of that! I know just what I can do and more important: what I cannot. At least not unless forced by circumstances . . .

A.G.: You suffer from a serious excess of humility . . . But I understand what you mean when you speak of a Master—because that was what friendship has most of all been in my own life, and every sudden turn that I've taken in one direction or the other has been necessitated by following some friend, to make or keep myself worthy of him . . . In my attempts at being a Communist I was driven more than anything else by the desire not to disappoint people I admired. Jef Last particularly— the moment I saw him at a demonstration he became so deeply important to me . . . What an astonishing fellow! His halo doesn't differ so much from your friend's— although Jef's an atheist. What devotion! Fire! Generosity . . . He never has a penny even though he's a best-seller in Holland, because around him are always a host of Comrades without bed and board and he takes care of them . . . He has been everything . . . He knows all the languages of the world . . . Once I took him on a trip to cheer him up, the Pyrenees, and the least brook, every snowy crag delighted him. I was bowled over. Hadn't he been round the world several times when he was a sailor? "Sure," he replied, "but always in the hold and without permission to land."

C.M.: Don't you miss at all having been deprived of the difficulties a Jef Last has known?

A.G.: I've worried about that . . . I even attempted to escape from this embarrassment! *Hélas!* What's the use of cheating? What good do you do not spending money if you *have* money? Nothing prevents people like ourselves from being *saved*. There's a separate exit for us. To wish to forget that is silly . . .

C.M.: But if it no longer exists, if like Jef Last one joins the International Brigade, if one accepts the risk of dying . . .

A.G.: That's true. But even there, what abuses! Circumstances exist in which going on living is more difficult than dying. My friend Father Doncoeur and I got into a heated discussion on just this point. Father

Doncoeur is another man with a real halo and I love and admire him, very much. In a book of his—I found it on my wife's bedside table though God knows how it got there—he spoke of the disappointment the Armistice caused many young men who were ready to go to the front. "What a beautiful chance to die we've lost!"

C.M.: There are a great many like that. Recall the last lines of Jacques' journal, about Munich: he too used that word, *disappointment.*

A.G.: Those words precisely made me think of Father Doncoeur.

C.M.: But in his case there is a reason of a religious nature. While the young men you were speaking of, like the large majority of Frenchmen, and especially those of bourgeois background, saw in war not so much an occasion for death as for devotion. One has to accord them this, a heroic courage in the fact of death—1914 proves it . . .

A.G.: And that's precisely what I won't stand for! In this world devoured by misery, there are so many occasions for sacrifice, and not just *useless* sacrifice . . .

C.M.: True . . . But I can't help thinking of those who *don't even have that courage* (unreasonable and stupid as it is): to calmly accept the idea of war, and the risk of death!

A.G.: I think I'm catching on . . . Now don't protest . . . And since we are about to part (but we'll meet again at Pontigny this summer perhaps, perhaps at Cuverville), there's something I want to tell you—since all I have for you cannot be compliments and how shall I say it? You seem to me . . . This is very hard to put . . . Well, here goes. I am shocked by your lack of appetite when it comes to cultivating yourself. I've watched your reactions to music and literature. *Real culture begins at the point where we approach what we don't already like.* I mean reading the book that didn't appeal to us from the first sentence or listening to a piece that didn't move us immediately. There and only there the enrichment begins. Now your friend Jacques always tries to understand something new—that impressed me. He has a large appetite for learning and loving. I'd like to see you that way. It will be too dreadful if people like yourself give up culture. We are headed faster and faster into a world in which it will be denied, neglected and made fun of. Who will save it if people worthy of it give it up too? Culture, I want you to realize, is something more than a personal pleasure. It shapes, it guides, it elevates . . .

C.M.: How right that it should be you that speaks to me this way! From this holiday spent near you, a great desire for enrichment and deepening are precisely what I'll bring back . . .

A.G.: I'm playing the schoolmaster . . . And I know perfectly well that no one has ever convinced anyone else of anything . . .

C.M.: And yet you have convinced me.

A.G.: I've reached the age when I want quiet. I often say to myself: Why go on reading? But you're not my age! I'm haunted by a phrase of Dostoievsky: "Don't sacrifice your life to nothing!" That is to say, remain available . . . In the name of that "availability" I condemn Father Doncoeur's young men. May you find in that phrase too reason to prefer culture to—

C.M.: Laziness!

A.G.: I didn't say that!

183

For a moment he collects his thoughts and then says, "I was thinking of which friend of mine I should introduce you to—as a Master. None of them will do. Not that I undervalue them, or you, but I don't think you and they go together . . ." Silence. Then, "Our conversations over the last few days have also been precious to me for another reason: they enter into the work on my play. They have stimulated me . . . In the same way your friend's journal stimulated me the other night—to work on the article about Claudel and the refugees . . . How *important* my stay at Malagar was! And how useful it was, how useful for *both* of us, don't you think? And wasn't it because I was able to *learn* who you are, your father and you? We could have gone on running into each other for years and never *learned* anything about each other."

And he walked off, having made up his mind, he said, to work a little.

Before lunch I saw him in the salon reciting a poem to Miss Adams, who corrected his pronunciation from time to time, Keats, eighty lines by heart . . .

"How long did it take you to learn that?" young Michel asked him in astonishment.

"Three years . . ."

And as he recited this poem I could not understand, fervent attention in his warm and tender voice, I admired him . . . No, he hasn't given up cultivating himself, this old man with a young man's heart always and a young man's face still . . . My father walks into the middle of the recitation. Doubtless he too was as astonished.

While I write this a torrential rain beats the panes of my window. I can hear brief howls, muffled cries: it is Gide, after his nap, playing chess with Mme. de Lestrange. I picture him as he looked last night, and the night before last before he read to us: considering out loud the pros and the cons, hesitating, playing after long delays, taking his move back, playing it over again, sighing, clearing his throat just to shout when his opponent moved her rook or her knight, "Oh, now, that is annoying! What am I to do?"—he coughs, sighs, his face screwed up by the effort of concentration; his unoccupied hand plays upon the green baize with whatever it comes upon . . .

In Châtellerault with Mme. de Lestrange, Gide and my father. A sad July 14th in this sad town. Gide is charming when our hostess teases him gently. He is such a spoiled child! But he accepts his friend's affectionate raillery with a smile.

Night brought an insipid display of fireworks to the village but it enchanted little Michel. Gide in a cape stood out against the short-lived stars. He and my father recited patriotic verse and *Les Châtiments* . . .

Saturday / July 15, 1939

Gide comes down to have breakfast with us. How sad he seems at the moment of our departure . . . That way he

185

has of shaking hands, almost on the sly, his body turned away a little . . . He decided not to accompany us to Paris, where he has nothing to do. But he says he'll miss the trip there with us . . .

Paris, Sunday / July 16, 1939

Saw Jean Davray. I told him about Gide's visit. I report things to him that I mention I haven't included in my journal and he scolds me. Among them, these words, said the other day in Chitré, in my room: "First of all not to allow oneself to become fascinated by the problems of the flesh. A day in my life finally arrived when I said to myself: Enough! Love, or better say, pleasure, shall torture me no longer. I give myself up without remorse to it." And this, from the end of our conversation on my lack of appetite for culture: "At bottom, there's no reason I know of for my giving you advice. Nothing is more vain. Each follows his own way. Each of us ought to. All intervention is useless. All of it is harmful." Davray was angry that I should have left out that appellation my father invented for Gide and used all the time, and once even in his presence: "Our demonic doctor . . ." And also this confession: "For a long time my curiosity tortured me. I always wanted to know what was behind the wall, over the horizon, on the other side of the mountain. I've ended by renouncing this pursuit. I did so when I realized it was in vain, that the unknown only pulled back a little when I advanced and stayed as inaccessible . . ."

And finally, this struck me as a sign—the only one—characteristic of his advanced age: his inability to date any of his memories, even the most recent. He recalls the place and the exact words of conversations he had there, but can't say whether before the war or after. He believes he visited Chitré last spring—it was last summer, etc. . . .

Thursday / July 27, 1939

Gide writes from Mont-Dore, where he's gone for a cure, that the day after we left Chitré, Saint-Exupéry and Guillaumet arrived "fresh from America. Terribly sorry that you weren't still here." He adds, "I still have my heart in my boots." As for my father, he received a long letter and, like mine, it was devoted almost entirely to our possible stay at Pontigny together. But he also wrote,

The most amazing thing is that you have been able to find something to thank me for! I'm cross with myself for allowing you to write me before I'd written you. My mother, who attached such importance to proper behavior—*"lettres de château"* and *"visites de digestion"*—would be pained to learn that I have remained so rude in spite of all her efforts! She would have said, "Your friend, no matter, he's an artist too. But can you imagine what *Madame* Mauriac is going to think?" The truth of the matter is I've allowed myself once more to simply drift and that I've just barely gotten a grip on myself this second day of cure . . . Dear friend, I don't believe you

187

realize how much Malagar, your invitation, hospitality, affection, your constant attentions, meant to me at a point in my life when out of a deep *dés-espoir* I felt an almost physical necessity for clutching at something . . . Yes, the time spent at Malagar near you has been very important for me . . .

Saturday / July 29, 1939

In a recent letter Gide writes that the thought of seeing me again, so soon, at Pontigny delights him. "You will see that it will all be very fine." He adds, "And now I see that I'm going to have to write a preface for *Les Liaisons Dangereuses*. It is a commitment made more than a year ago and forgotten completely. Maurois writes that he answered for me, that the book has been announced (American publisher) and that there's no way I can get myself off the hook, etc. Awful drudgery! When I feel myself so little in the mood to write— anything at all, even this letter to you . . ."

PART FOUR

Pontigny

Pontigny, Sunday / August 13, 1939

Alone in the library with Gide. He leans over the table writing his preface for *Les Liaisons Dangereuses.* How young he seemed when he met me and what warmth at seeing me again I felt in his greeting! A real pleasure born of a real friendship: in me it provoked jealousy, a demand for a more genuine friendship—he could not have behaved more *affectionately*; but I wanted him even more friendly than that. I took a short walk and appeared again in the library. Gide's working still. He walks back and forth, sits down and thinks with his chin on one hand. He gets up again—his shoes squeak . . . He leafs through some books and sits down once more. I ask him if don't I get on his nerves. "Your mute presence, on the contrary . . ." All right.

"You know *Les Liaisons Dangereuses?*"

"I should hope so! That book has meant a lot to me . . ."

"Then you must realize what importance this preface has in my eyes . . ."

He stands out against the light behind him. Can I do better than watch him on the sly? His head only half erect is lost in shadow. Gide strikes a match. Since I got back from my walk he hasn't said a word. The book I went for bores me. I'm afraid I'd disturb him if I looked for another. Good excuse for spying on him. You'll admit that the experience is rare: surprising André Gide in the act of creation . . . But what a strange method of working he has! Twice he got up and left the library—for a minute. From time to time he heaves a sigh—one sigh. And those strange walks he takes . . .

In the library some time later Gide reads his preface to me. Robert L. came in just as he ended. I had just remarked to Gide that what always struck me in Valmont's character was his taste for gaming. He plays with love, he plays with hearts. That lets in the Devil (whom Gide rightly evokes) because one cannot play with creatures of flesh and blood unpunished. Gide supports my thesis by producing one of his notes he forgot to use, which says the same thing. He returns to his manuscript and adds a paragraph or two on this dangerous game. "I believe I've finished . . ." And the preface? Rather superficial—goes too fast.

Gide shows me a letter from Mme. Du Bos. He doesn't know what to do: she wants to see him. His was the last name on her dear Charlie's lips. She has a serious message from him for Gide. She is aware of his loathing for conventions but there are situations in which the convention would be—to refuse. "Don't try to escape!" she writes. And this pathetic letter bears the signature, "Zezette." Gide relates the case of the wife of his friend Laurens: she assured him that her dead husband spoke to her and demanded the conversion of Gide. "It's all going to begin again! What can I do?

Driven into such a corner, all that's left is moral treason! In the face of sorrow, what can I say or attempt?" He has that hunted look . . .

In the night along the walls of that squat church, innumerable couples hasten. Innumerable carnal attachments parallel spiritual attachments here, and dramas of the heart, and its joys with the joys and dramas of the intellect. Jankélévitch had told me beforehand, "Pontigny has a charm, a particular grace, a mystery." Marvelous room in the lodge on the ground floor. Marvelous for its woodwork but also marvelously uncomfortable . . . In the room above me, Gide's footsteps. He keeps me from sleep with his perpetual walking . . .

I misjudged Gide badly when I read that he had just mailed a most severe letter to Jouhandeau about his *l'Abjection.* ("Jouhandeau's book is stupefying! What a will to please he shows in his use of stench!" and in the next letter: "I have written rather severely to Jouhandeau—I'll show you a copy of the letter—and I expect a sensational reply!") How could I have allowed myself to be deceived? "The only complaint I have is the complexity he elicited from things in reality so simple. He does make mountains out of molehills and bother the poor Devil for almost nothing." Almost nothing! Homosexuality? Here one touches the weak place in this heart of his, otherwise so strictly consistent. How completely without defenses he is face to face with his own sin, dear Gide! He tries to convict it of "not counting." He tries to convince *himself.*

193

Monday / August 14, 1939

Down there I see Gide strolling near the corner. He walks into a building and comes right out, leans over the little stream, turns toward me, takes a note. All the while his head glistens in the sun. Here he is, smiles, and wiggles his fingers nervously. "They're typing my preface for me. I finished it this morning . . ." A little howl and he's gone.

Tomorrow the conference on aliens begins. Today already about twenty participants have arrived. Hideolas the lot! Conversations all morning with Robert Levesque, Doctor Sotty and a young (future) *Normalien,* Jean Curtis, eighteen. Good fun that lasts all day and well into the night. (Just now a charming little Norwegian girl with a pure fresh laugh joined us.) Simpleminded games that enchant us, for instance, inventing a poet, Jean Cheminée, and talking about no one else. That was to keep that learned, that encyclopedic bore W. from getting a word in edgewise. Gide's pockets turned out to be laden with little puzzles. He enjoys watching these young intellectuals worry over them and his patient watchfulness astonishes me as much as does their patient desire to overcome these obstacles. Of these little games (twisted nails, beebees which must be rolled in a certain order into small holes, and the like) he tells me the usefulness on trips if you want pretexts to make people's acquaintance . . .

Gide shows me a letter in which Henri Guillemin defends the way he pulled Flaubert into the Christian camp. "For almost four years Flaubert's *Letters* were my bedside book," Gide told me as we visited the gardens. "There I discovered to my amazement and reassurance that outside of religion another morality and another grandeur exist. And now they tell me that his ethic is that of Christ! This produces two contrary reactions in me: first anger, because it isn't true, and then more reassurance." Then he turns ironic suddenly: "So! I just said to myself: Let go, follow your bent. There's a Henri Guillemin waiting for you who'll explain how your bent was Christian!"

After dinner we talked about his preface. He isn't yet satisfied.

"I haven't formulated or I have badly formulated the most essential point. Meaning: the joy I experience reading a book that doesn't toe the current moral line."

"Very well. But you have labeled this work *hair-raising* from the first line . . ."

"It *is* hair-raising. It's important that I make clear how Valmont disturbs me. What a sorry end to such involved maneuvers, pitiful!"

"Yes, I'd like to say to him, 'You call that progress?' "

"There now! I ought to say that."

"Yes, it would be *decent* to do so. But they will turn this explication against you. They'll say, 'Gide recognizes that without religion one disintegrates, finds oneself alone, degenerates.' Thus you will have to sketch out your true position: not Valmont, Flaubert. Thus an occasion for you to answer that serious question Guillemin raises . . ."

"This will be difficult. But you may be right . . . I think I'll hang on to the manuscript a few more days . . ."

And he's off . . .

Midnight. I've just left Levesque, Sotty, Curtis and Robert L. The little Norwegian girl who has the room next to mine has just told me good night. Lovely voice. Over my head I can still hear Gide: from the depths of sleep he whines from time to time, baby noises and nothing sad about them.

Tuesday / August 15, 1939

Gide: "I apologize for the way I ran off last night but the things you said about *Liaisons* were *exciting*. I felt *full* again. The empty library enjoys a marvelous silence at that hour, so I went right to work. Ten minutes of perfect joy, consuming work. A lyrical feeling in creation that I experience so seldom nowadays . . . It's been a year since I've felt such enthusiasm. Sad that I should tire so quickly . . . The exaltation receded so suddenly . . ." He hands me his small notebook to read; the fruit of his nocturnal labor. I recognize our thoughts of the night before but insufficiently detailed. I tell him so. I add that in speaking of *ennui* he diminishes the intensity of the hopelessness in which Valmont's solitude ends. Or he must be using *ennui* in the seventeenth-century sense. He objects that he has denied himself the whole *mystical* vocabulary in this preface and I have to admit he was right to. He on the other hand agrees that his text must be strengthened. It will be. "But on the other hand," he adds, "I have no desire to be the Guillemin of Laclos." Last of all: "What seems in the end to have been the most important feature of *Les Liaisons Dangereuses* is the dissociation Laclos makes between pleasure and love. This corresponds almost exactly with the code I have drawn up for my own life . . ." That explains why he mentions none of this in his preface—it would involve overburdening it with explanations.

He shows me a letter from Jean Paulhan suggesting an issue of the *NRF* devoted to his life and works. He begs off humbly. I object that gidism has surpassed itself to infinity, lost in the spread of Gide himself, that it really was time, after all, for further clarification.

Jean Davray arrived on the noon bus. What pleasure in greeting him and initiating him into the routine of Pontigny. Gide up on his balcony and looking young—incredibly—waves to us. "Thirty-five," Jean says. He hardly exaggerates.

Three o'clock. Mme. Desjardins opens the conference. Then I introduce our committee for the rural settlement of Spanish refugees. In the following discussion Gide suggests a rather timid resolution. W. inexhaustible, catastrophically omniscient . . .

In Jean-Marie's car our little group drove as far as the dam in hopes of a swim but gave up. Coming back we picked up Gide, who was strolling on the road: the car starts up with the Master crowded in with laughing young people. Gide pulls out those horrible little puzzles. Teasers whose ravages he never tires of watching. For some minutes we drive ourselves wild trying to separate those demonic nails, wound around one another, which Gide, who knows their trick, can undo with one twist.

Before dinner Davray and I visit Gide in his room. "I had finished that preface, but as we talked Claude opened new horizons for me. I realized that I had to dig deeper. The trouble at the moment is I have not succeeded in expressing or at least in arranging what has to be added . . ." Then, manuscript in hand, he asks our help in locating the point where he could decently slip in such a paragraph he now feels indispensable.

The whole evening Gide perseveres with his puzzles. Ah! If it weren't he . . .

Wednesday / August 16, 1939

Arrival of old Desjardins.

Not at all busied with Gide today. This morning he was dying to go with us to Vézelay, that was clear, but at the same time some obscure reason prevented him—it fits in with his character. During the discussion he joins in, but cautiously.

Thursday / August 17, 1939

In his room again Gide reads us the final version of his preface. He admits himself, "I've said nothing, been *able* to say nothing about the essential results of my conversations with Claude." Indeed, there's almost nothing on "the game," and nothing that disavows Valmont clearly, nothing on the *particular* Satanism of his schemes, nothing on the Moral of Flaubert against the A-moral of Valmont. In spite of that there are some details of importance contributed by our conversations. And once more Gide adds a commentary: "I will never be able to express in one introduction everything that I intend. Where can I *put* the most important remarks? How can I weld them to what I've already written? I've drawn nothing but the outline of the subject: I explain everything around it but I haven't gotten to its essentials, itself . . ."

Then this confession whose scope seems to escape him —because it implicitly recognizes his failings as novelist and critic: "I'll escape by publishing these notes *separately*. As a journal perhaps. That's the way I express myself most truly. *It is easier than trying to fashion a single work.*"

The reading over, he left for the library to hunt up a Lautréamont and show us that "a similar *twist* shapes *Les Liaisons* and *Les Chants de Maldoror*." That was a strange session . . . Behind his dark glasses Jean Davray's eyes expressed horror and delight at once. Gide read with his deepest voice. It was beautiful. Up to the moment it became embarrassing . . . How can I describe this clearly? Gide became suddenly the Devil's tool. His voice found new harmonies, more persuasive, lulling, insinuating, more *perfide* than usual. His features shone with evil rapture. I could no longer admire him. I was afraid. Of course the scene was picturesque: not every day do we hear that awful passage read in which Maldoror writes to Mervyn—and certainly not by André

199

Gide. Davray perceived the gamy side as well as I. But we were cast ashore far beyond such poor sensations.

What had become of our charming Gide with all his propriety, our attentive Gide with his affection, goodness and wit, the Gide we loved? Maldoror's letter and Mervyn's answer—the man reading these is animated by what evil joy? I'm going to copy out here a few lines that will reveal this "other face of André Gide." They must be imagined, I repeat, joined to his emphatic accent, with a totally new face, new tone of voice and repertoire of gestures. Every word appeared surrounded with a bouquet of fireworks, every word poured forth, flew like an arrow and hit: " '. . . Young *man, I am interested in you,* I want to make you *happy.* I will take you for a *companion* and we will make long peregrinations among the isles of Ocean. *Mervyn, you know that I love you* and I have no *need* of *proving* it to you. *You will give me your friendship, of that I am sure.* I shall become your *brother* and you shall not lack for *good counsel. Young man,* I salute you . . .' " I have italicized the words and phrases in this text (already completely and profoundly "italicized" by Gide's biblical voice) which came in for even greater emphasis.

At dinner we discover that Mme. Desjardins has arranged the places differently. I am no longer in disgrace. Not at all. "Disgrace" in our language means sitting far from wherever Gide sits. Again the astonishing youth of his face, disturbing: below that immense forehead his little eyes, mere slits, opened like almonds and sparkling with mischief. His face has a certain heaviness toward the bottom. But irony, pleasure, joy all light it up, regenerate it, save it. Illuminated features, features of Gide! "He looks like a Buddha!" the girl next to me says. How right if you add an unexpected epithet: ascetic!

This place makes me happy: in it old and young are united in one fervor by the conspiring of intellect, and culture. Paul Desjardins seems so easy to like. He moves me. Already I want to please and have already succeeded: I let my good spirits do the talking. No, I've seldom seen better books nor books better chosen. The abbey is noble and so are its owners. I'm already in love with Mme. Desjardins; brave, charitable, active, she directs her seventy guests with gentle authority. (With what gusto she directed each guest to his place before dinner!) Voice a bit hoarse, face of stone beneath hair black on one side and white on the other, separated as neatly as brick ice cream.

Gide's sleep is musical tonight as every night. He plays little elegies that melt into the night. Those little puzzles of his would have driven me mad if I'd allowed myself to notice . . .

Friday / August 18, 1939

Paul Desjardins keeps to the sidelines. No one pays him any mind. The activities of his wife encircle his passivity. Is it possible that he doesn't realize he's in the way? Devoted as she is to him, she is hard, without noticing, she's so hurried. And she has a way of behaving as though he's no one or not there . . . She walks fast, dragging me with her, and the poor old man gives up very quickly . . . She makes it clear he's not wanted when for some reason or other he walks into an office where we're working. Timidly he excuses himself and goes. Pontigny is his creation. What sadness in the falling off of age! Lucid but a little slow, he is charmingly sweet and humble. And Pontigny lives and breathes all around him with a life he has given it, and pays him not the least attention.

Trophinoff, piano teacher, follows Gide's advice as best he can. Gide behind him explains: "No one knows how to *read* Chopin. This prelude has its *raison d'être* in that difference of meter which you are not observing. The right hand . . . While the left hand . . ." Then all sorts of technicalities which I am not musician enough to understand, but which Gide's good student tries to assimilate.

During the course of the discussions a young Czech speaks for his people in exile. Davray for the German Jews. Gide takes the floor as well. And he excites admiration, caring about anyone else, at his age. Fatiguing bicycle ride with Robert L. The evening light transforms ripe grain fields and the underbrush. The new smells here in the country wash me clean, to rebirth and a wholeness.

After dinner, in front of the assembled conference, Gide reads his *Bethsabé*. The rich and powerful voice hammers out the grave poetry of this work. Seated somewhat at an angle Gide turns now and then from the book which lies open on the table and recites a long sentence from memory, his eyes closed. His voice acts out the story, fills it with the desire, tenderness, loneliness and distress of David, its hero. The magnificence of the Bible is not easily distinguished in this story from Gide's own contribution.

The old Scandinavian Syndicalist, Backlund, sitting on the edge of his chair so that the table bears his full weight, does not seem any more interested in this reading than he is in that bad leg of his lying strangely like an abandoned rag-doll there on the carpet. He's dozing. This isn't his show. On the other hand, André Philip looks fascinated. Jean Curtis (who is reading *Nourritures Terrestres* for the first time) listens, standing; his whole heart is in it. (Toward the end he found an ironic look necessary.) Levesque, turned to stone with admiration, remains motionless, the lollipop he'd chosen (on our example) held a good inch from his mouth. Dutch, Germans, English, Hungarians, Czechs—they may not understand what's going on but they hold their breaths. Collective good behavior: during the whole reading no one lit a cigarette—nor were they warned not to. "I'm not satisfied," Gide told me afterwards. "The good in it I borrowed from the Bible. I don't care for this style that's neither fish nor fowl. And nowadays I've such a horror of overemphasis . . ."

Later we took a night walk with him, in the company of Robert Levesque, Jean Davray, Jean Curtis and Robert L. We didn't act our age. It's clear that Gide prefers this to the often indiscreet questions of some of those here. And then it's always a pleasure for him, having young men around him.

203

Saturday / August 19, 1939

What can I say about a day like today? Gide ever attentive—in an ecstasy—to those who allow themselves to be trapped into the disaster of those puzzles. A deadly long speech by André Philip on the laws regarding aliens. The arrival of the Italian Socialist Rossi, who writes for the *Populaire* under the name Leroux. A bicycle ride with Levesque and Curtis. A reading by Gide, everybody present, of his *Enfant Prodigue.* Between Gide and myself the simplest relations, cordial, natural. Not a serious word, not even an attempt at one. A trivial and agreeable talk during which I feel no need to "make him talk," much less sparkle.

Old Desjardins makes a great effort during a private conversation to answer Philippe Serre, who was stating the case of the *Normaliens*: that only a jurist will know how to adapt himself to the changes which facts make in theories. This very questionable hypothesis is left unquestioned by Desjardins. He sticks to a single point: that the question itself is invalid because it supposes a group of people, interchangeable members, called *Normaliens,* and in reality there are many sorts. Under a big beret a tiny face grows an unkempt beard, all white in wisps. He speaks slowly and with difficulty. His words come from far away. But they do come, well thought out, intelligent. I'm rather dazzled. I think of the treasures of culture that sleep in this old head which death will soon wipe out. I think of the sorrow of growing old! He reasons as well as he ever did in his life, but the moderator, quicker for his years, never allows him time to collect his thoughts. Just this once they all gather round him. They are listening. He names names. Those of his classmates. Just these names are enough to assure his point victory: Bergson, Durkheim, Jaurès . . . He mentions too that he was sixteen in 1870. He adds that for three years he attended the lectures of Fustel de Coulanges. A name like that puts a man far back in the past, yet here he is alive, before us . . .

During dinner Gide with a seductive look presents the girl next to me one of his diabolical puzzles. The young lady is caught immediately. I come up with a very "literary" dictum that gives reality that finishing touch so dear to Jean Davray (who, by the way, hears allusions and ambiguities in every word Gide says): "And he passes out toys to the girls to get their minds off the boys." What a malicious joy Jean finds in repeating Gide's *bon mots* and what perverse ingenuity he expends in interpreting his glances! "Wanting Gide more Gide than life offers, betrays one and the other, Gide and life."

A pretty young Swedish girl who's here with her whole family has barely mixed with the rest of us, she knows so little French. She seemed to be so discouragingly icy in regard to me that for some time now I've satisfied myself with our morning hello. It was useless trying to stir any emotion from her beautiful but impassive features. But in the rearranged seating at dinner tonight she appeared next to me and turned out to be as talkative and gay as she was not *marmorean*. Her name is Selma. We took a walk together with Jean Curtis. Nothing happened on our walk except that she gained more and more confidence as it got darker and darker. My room opens directly on the garden. We go there since the afternoon rain still wets all the benches. Seated all three on one sofa. Curtis's presence saves me from my imprudent self. But he's bored to death. In vain I plead with him for poetry. He yawns. Upstairs Gide, probably just fallen asleep, sighs. We have to keep very still not to wake him. How the scent of that smooth face without cosmetics appeals to me! That tenderness, that peacefulness, that nonchalance a woman exudes the moment a man's face has become to her the most serious mystery . . . After our conversation, which her imperfect French made difficult, complete understanding. Man and Woman: the only really live *Internationale*. Beyond all mere civilization, all differences ethnic or racial, we found one another, faithful to a rendez-vous made at the beginning of time, mysteriously, and reunited finally, united in the greatest and oldest understanding.

At midnight I had to return her to her mother. Our silent kisses did not disturb Curtis, who blurted out naïvely that he didn't see how we kept still that long. "How could you keep her here like that?" he asked when we were alone again. "Were you really unaware that she was every bit as bored as I was on that sofa?"

Monday / August 21, 1939

Gide on Desjardins: "You see him slowed down now. But in the old days when he was still young and the machine was well oiled and started in at nine every morning, he was something to see! Such complexes, such spitefulness; with these he created a character right out of Corneille. He would watch himself from the time he got up, playing out a comedy, his comedy . . . You'd see him in the vestibule on all fours picking up cigarette butts as a sign of protest against his guests, and that just ten minutes before the servants were due to clean the place. It was Copeau first of all who pointed out how remarkable Desjardins really was. With more culture than anybody and at the same time so spiteful, so biting, a bit soured by not having the position he deserved, he had instead the most awful insolence! Every drop of talent he had went into teaching. As for his written work, he was never able to bring himself to declare it finished, tormented in this area by some weird impotence . . ."

Bicycle ride with Robert L. Important conversation over a few pages of these notes I'd loaned him. The joy physical exercise releases after haggling in committee animated both of us. The intimate questions he asks I answer without effort, my mind unrolling what I know as easily as my legs turn the pedals. What sort of answers? For as long as I can remember homosexuality has been simply unthinkable as far as I was concerned, but at the same time I'd never felt the least revulsion for homosexuals personally. That as far as I was concerned there was no "moral problem"—if I were that way it's exactly what I'd do and thus I don't condemn them, but nonetheless: I am not that way!

The persuasiveness of my irony, the severity of my accent was such that Robert didn't for a minute doubt me. But he was startled that I had never had so frank and *decisive* a talk with Gide . . . "He would be quite surprised," he tells me, "and *annoyed*! His reading *Maldoror* the other day—I'm sure from things you said, and Davray too, and certain allusions by Gide himself— was nothing more than an experiment. An experiment on you! He meant to disturb you."

"Disturb *me?*"

"No doubt about it. Now how annoyed he'd be if he heard from your own lips that you were disturbed, but by the evil in his face, not the evil in what he had chosen to read."

"Oh no! He only wanted to illustrate a parallel with *Les Liaisons!*"

"A pretext, no doubt about it . . . Gide loves to disturb people. He loves to please people. He's certain you're 'vulnerable.' "

And we kept pedaling down that moist road. Mists rose from the ground. In a hurt tone of voice (distressed at the notion that I'd been made a fool of) I said, "Disturb me with *Maldoror!* That's childish . . . Gide himself has taught us never to be shocked at anything. '*De quels rayons se vêtait ma gloire'* in *Si le Grain ne meurt* has once and for all made such amazement an—impossibility."

And I added with bitterness: "I'm fond of Gide . . . I was . . . I have confidence in him . . . Or did . . ."

Looking inward I caught sight of Gide's face: slightly sardonic, it radiated an evil joy.

This countenance is mixed up in the odd evening that followed. I experienced every drop of distress and joy a particular mystery has to offer . . . To the eyes of the uninitiated what would that after-dinner gathering have been? Everyone who had a number performed: one sang an English song (or was it Dutch?), another recited a poem—in Swedish; a third read some Goethe, another God-knows-what in Hungarian, two joined forces for some scenes from *Macbeth*, Trophinoff interpreted Liszt, Govin played the flute, Gide recited with willful overemphasis one of *Les Fleurs du Mal*, old Desjardins read from Dante's *Inferno* with tremulous voice, and Mlle. B., who is known as *la Seiche* (bone of cuttlefish you see in bird cages) because W. has been sharpening his teeth on her, sang in Italian . . . What can I add but that the heights of the sublime were reached and the depths of the grotesque too . . . It was "Pontigny," all of it, and the particular charm of the place.

But there was something else. Photograph albums were brought out and the Pontigny of the old days came to life before my eyes. The past mixed with the present, one overlapping the other here and there. Such anguish clutched me. How can I describe it? I had never seen these photographs of my father as a young man. I never saw my father as a young man . . . He was laughing, in the company of Gide, Fernandez. His clothes looked slightly unfashionable. Lacretelle was there too. And Georges Duhamel. All of them hard to recognize: I recognized the triumphant youth of these gentlemen I've only known with worn faces. But Paul Desjardins on the other hand appeared in these ancient photographs no different than I see him tonight. He's no older in appearance. Not by a year . . . Time seems abolished: under these very trees that I can recognize this day, another age entertained and loved. And I was jealous of my father! Jealous of Gide, whose face in his youth there in the old Pontigny was even more Mephistophelean. I compared the two men, the one in the photographs with a disturbing sweetness in his almond eyes, the one across from me, his face hardly thickened at all since then—and suddenly, thanks to the one the other gave up its real meaning. He grew younger before my very eyes, this man whose movements are the same today as the day the camera brought them into focus more than twenty years ago, and the photographs aged there in my hands; the two became one and I was afraid of I don't know what.

Tuesday / August 22, 1939

Coup de théâtre: the Soviet Union with whom the Franco-English "Peace Front" has been negotiating for so many months has just signed a nonaggression pact with the Reich. Confusion: clustered around the radio we couldn't believe our ears. Philippe Serre declares that after this master stroke any resistance to Hitler in Poland has become meaningless; France must withdraw to "rethink" the situation. Madame Desjardins fights stoically against her discouragement: "I lost a son in the war," she says, "and yet Munich was the greatest suffering I've gone through."

Wednesday / August 23, 1939

Morning of work with Gide, Curtis, Levesque in the library. Contradictory reports. Neither France nor England has reacted officially. In the great hall of the abbey Robert L. reads excitedly from his journal: outside it's raining, inside Gide listens. It is the journal of their trip to Greece. I'll return to this if there is time . . . The confusion of the papers is at its most appalling.

Thursday / August 24, 1939

White posters on the walls of the post office. Numbers beginning three and four have been called up. Blasé. Not the thunderous effect of last September but all the same . . . Chatter. Dread. The conference ends sadly.

Departure, with most of the guests, on the narrow gauge at 1:00 P.M. Gide, Desjardins and the few who're remaining accompanied us to the station. Gide, suddenly very moved by the moment of parting, kisses me on both cheeks. Thought about Selma with breaking heart: never seeing her again.

Malagar, Wednesday / August 30, 1939

We have talked a great deal about Gide these last days between two air-raid warnings. Events have so far prevented my going into detail on the subject of Robert L.'s reading of his journal, in which one sees Gide and him hunting "adventures" in the mountains of Greece. Since an apparent slowdown in events (such as we know them) has left my mind relatively free this morning, I shall try to work out my new conception of André Gide.

Because what I think of him has changed. I did not realize this at once, the evolution insensibly working itself out. What did he mean to me before the conference at Pontigny? A Master. I mean I'd taken him as a model. Not so much in the realm of literature as in the realm of the spirit. I knew of his "morals." I knew them to be different from my own. No matter, since what alone had importance for me was the consistent manner with which sincerity and courage filled his life. My own life was differently oriented than his. But such sincerity and courage could lend it nobility. Thus I admired André Gide. More than that, I loved him. His attentiveness, his wholeheartedness moved me, and what I found in his make-up of the too-sensitive, the too-tender. I had no doubts about having found in him, in spite of his age, in spite of his fame, a true friend, someone devoted, strong, understanding, on whom I could call in difficult times.

Now what changes in this point of view did the stay at Pontigny make? I am unable to tell with much clarity. But there was a decided change. I will always love and admire André Gide. But I do love and admire him in a different way. As for the mutual trust and understanding, I'm not so sure. As the source of my disappointment, perhaps I can put Gide's attitude to our group of young people, that way he had of stalking around us with suspicious envy. But what do I hold against him in this? Nothing tangible. Gide was aware that he has prestige in our eyes and he wanted our company. He always showed good taste and tact. His coquetry was never free from touchiness: he always feared he was intruding. Since he didn't dare come nearer he smiled enigmatically from a distance. Or he would join us but we felt he was nervous, likely to fly off suddenly like a half-trained bird. Indifferent but at the same time—jealous. I realize that it is impossible to express such distinctions in one's grievances . . . To make a long story short, I found that Gide was not as *strong* as I'd supposed him, and much more vulnerable. To tell the truth, I should have known this and I did, but I did not *feel* it. I knew of the thorn in his flesh, the suspicions his heart keeps always alive. I did not realize that this vulnerability could transform itself into all those poor, timid actions, all the proud humility of his bearing, so *feminine* in the end, so incompatible with the dignity of the *man*.

What do I have against Gide? A lack of good taste and modesty in spite of his apparently excessive good taste and modesty. He lacks that profound severity with himself without which no man has real grandeur. His exterior intransigence hides a heart which is ever disposed to compromise. With this I have not accused the exquisite friend, the admired writer, the man of heart and taste, but the *maître*. Perhaps it was his prestige which Gide lost for me at Pontigny. And by that perhaps I have said "what made him especially dear to me."

One scene decided everything for me. Without it I would have perhaps never found the meaning in so many imponderable warnings. It took place on August 23 in the great hall. It was raining and that great vaulted room with its contemplative silence invited work and solitude nostalgically. Robert L. read me his journal. Could anything have prepared me for such crude coarseness? How could I have known beforehand that this man with his laughing baby face, but humble, reserved, tasteful manner, was capable of such passion? And more precisely, of a passion which sent him off chasing young shepherds? Undressed, on a hill not far from Athens, they knew the delights of love, of Greek love, I ought to say.

Robert showed at least the remains of modesty when he refused to allow Jean Curtis to attend this reading. Eighteen, think of it! But Jean Curtis came back to beg. After a while Gide appeared in his suspicious way, with his curiosity. How he carried on before he decided to stay for the second section which Robert announced: the part of their Easter journey that he had not yet read

214

to even Gide himself. It was clear from the beginning that Gide would remain. But he made us plead with him. He played Modesty Warned, Sensuality in Confusion. He feigned several attempts at departure. He spoke of his "embarrassment." His eyes sparkled with mischief. After he was finally seated, Robert asked Jean Curtis to leave. The poor child refused energetically. "You are too young . . . I refuse to assume the responsibility . . ."

"You really think so?" asked Gide with a voice so sweetly smooth that I felt a little sick.

"I do! There are some very daring passages . . ."

Gide's hands indicate delight. "What's the difference?" he asks. "On the contrary!" He insists that Curtis stay. But Robert and I manage to get him out. Gide gives in.

Unforgettable session. Gide listens, his cheek sunk over the fingers of one hand, eyes half closed. Robert's muffled voice never hesitates at any boldness. Nothing else comes up but little boys, looking for them and finding them. During Holy Week they don't hesitate to enter churches to ferret them out. "I'm leaving out nothing—so much the worse!" Robert interjects between two sentences. Everything? For instance: "Gide, to catch sight of him again, pretended to be thirsty. We went in . . ." Or: "He took the boy and offered him to Gide." Gide is not embarrassed, nor Robert. I conceal my amazement. From time to time Gide interrupts with particulars. No, the sky was not blue that day, there was no running water, just water; that is a most unfortunate sentence and he prefers something more concrete . . .

Robert makes corrections humbly. Gide congratulates him: he didn't take any notes himself during those marvelous days. He's happy someone did it for him.*

There were some very beautiful passages. For instance, one in which a Greek boy kisses Gide's hand, Gide who must represent something special to him in that place and at that time when war menaces Greece— the Italian conquest of Albania. Something beautiful and noble? "France itself!" Gide qualifies. "It was simply that I was French that made him kiss my hand. You don't bring that out sufficiently. You have mentioned that the goats had 'lyrical horns,' but that's not quite it, they ought to be 'biblical.' But as a whole the narrative is right as to form and tone. Congratulations. That was the day which of all my days made me feel closest to Antiquity. I returned that kiss. I kissed the boy's hand! What a mistake! I could tell that from his disappointed face, poor child. What he expected from me was a blessing. And like a fool I played the friend!"

* Gide wrote me on March 11, 1940, "Nothing has brought me any pleasure recently except a long letter from Robert L. He has copied out the whole story of our trip to Greece last year. Will I ever again know such a carefree existence?"

PART FIVE

After the
Liberation

December 13, 1944, my father received the following letter from Algiers:

My dear Mauriac,

I want you to know with what attention, what passionate interest and what approbation of mind and heart we follow, Anne Heurgon and myself, every article of yours we can procure—and often it is very difficult to do so. What comfort they are so often able to give us! Anne Heurgon meant to write you but has put it off from day to day, overburdened as she is with household tasks. Thanks to her care I have not suffered excessively from this exile which will surely last into the Spring—until the climate in France, materially as well as emotionally, becomes a little more clement. But I have longed greatly to see certain friends again.

You are too busy to write me and have better things to do I am sure—but Claude perhaps . . . I haven't heard a thing from him or about him. If he only knew the pleasure a word or two from him would give me! Please assure him (if he is in Paris) of my deep affection, and as for you, dear friend, never doubt that I remain most faithfully,

Yours,
André Gide.

Among my papers I found the draft of a letter I wrote him later:

Paris, January 14, 1945

Dear André Gide,

I shall not attempt to find excuses for this silence which has prolonged itself so greatly, even though events would have allowed me to break it several months ago. I am hardly yet awake, like every other Frenchman, from the amazement of Liberation and all the ups and downs that came with it or followed. To tell the truth, I have never stopped thinking about you all through the interminable years, nor about the miracle of our friendship. And one of the joys of our deliverance is the possibility of seeing you again. If I have not yet done so, it is first of all, as I have said, due to the bewildering life I've led since August and again due to a sort of powerless feeling. I have realized that what separates me from you much more than any merely material obstacle is *me*, and you yourself. So rapid and so brief were the months of our friendship, and so long drawn-out the years that preceded and followed its birth and development, that I shall never again be able, completely, to believe in its existence. Even now I have to make an effort to break the spell . . .

But I ought not put off any longer writing you these few words and this first of all: that your place awaits you, as do all your friends who have been unanimous, rightly, in adjudging the accusations of Aragon dishonest. But to speak frankly, in spite of the great desire I have of seeing you again, I do not advise your immediate return: passions are at their height, blood has given birth to blood, hate to hate; these poison and dishonor the pure joy and marvelous happiness of the first days of a liberated France. Death, in whose company the least heroic of us lived during the Occupation, is still here as much as ever at our sides. More than ever we must live on familiar terms with death, and I do not refer simply to those under arms as I am not. The worst threats have met my father. But I am not afraid. All of my thoughts, however, cannot help but be to a certain extent those of a changed person. No, stay where you are if you can, beyond the reach of this madness. From where you are these events must already appear with some historical distance and not just their distance in space—perhaps you can see their greatness.

Thus the fantastic days of Paris's liberation have come and gone, in which I participated with as little thought as any man in the street. "The street" in my case was the one where I happened to be, not the one where I live. At the barricade on the Pont-Neuf I knew the most powerful joy I've ever lived through, only to have it surpassed by my first meeting with General de Gaulle.

Because this is what happened: my friend Claude Guy, about whom I worried every day for four years, had become the aide-de-camp of the General, and he appealed to me for help their first night in Paris because the General had arrived ahead of everyone else, almost alone. It was thus that I took part so totally in the historic hours which followed. And that having accepted the post with the understanding that it was temporary (since I felt myself completely unqualified) and to bail out a friend. I find myself at time of writing still a member of the General's cabinet, as chief of his private secretariat.

For us de Gaulle was a voice and a myth. And here am I by pure chance living on familiar terms with him. He made such an impression on me, the joy the Liberation freed was so overwhelming, one thing happened after another and so miraculously, that I lived in the most

221

exalted of dreams the first few months of our deliverance. Overworked, of course, completely out of touch with myself, but all the same unable to snuff out completely in myself that lucidity and rigor which will prevent me to the very end of being the absolute dupe of any passion or idea whatsoever.

That time has passed. And I must admit now that in that miraculous adventure, which was the salvation of France, there were imperfections which no human enterprise escapes from. The death sentences, miscarriages of justice, lies of politicians, hypocrisy, the weakness of institutions and the baseness of mankind, every shame of every age was reborn, and I feel that in my small way I am responsible, and in my heart of hearts hear this word: "Traitor!" But in the name of France—and it is myself I have betrayed—and because it is for France, this land which in spite of everything has again revived, and because France must be born anew beautiful and strong and great from this mire, I cannot regret it. Nor in my actions had I any choice . . . A moment arrives when we cannot any longer refuse employment, when it is necessary to make up one's mind to play the game.

You will understand these matters, you without a doubt the man who taught me intellectual honesty as you taught it to several generations, who schooled more than one generation in a lesson which would have made their happiness eternal if they had only known how to apply it. But lies and bad faith have never before been so widespread—see Aragon's article.

As long as the Germans appeared to be winning the war, our existence was living death. In the Europe which they assured us was "being born" I knew perfectly well that there was no place for me and that I would never again be able to bring myself to publish a line. And for a long time after their defeat was a certainty, the Nazi stayed on here. And it was still necessary that we hold our tongues, and from holding our tongues we forgot we could talk. For my part I forgot after a time that it was because of specific circumstances and a choice of my own that I was living so obscurely. So much so that the full light of liberty and what it revealed of myself came as a shock. Indeed, every day I am still surprised that I fulfill some social function and do so no worse than many others.

Forgive me for speaking so much of myself. But what else could you have expected? And I have only said a small portion of all that I have to tell you. Four years in the life of a thirty-year-old, and years of such weight; they add up . . .

I am filled with the most ardent wishes on your behalf at the opening of this year 1945, as yet so ominous with threats, and I embrace you with all my old fraternal and respectful affection.

Claude Mauriac

André Gide answered from Algiers, February 3, 1945:

My dear Claude,

If your excellent letter, heralded by your father and avidly expected (dated January 4th, it didn't arrive until this morning, February 3rd!) was late in getting here, to compensate (or *"en récompense,"* as they said in the seventeenth century) I shall answer at once and without letting that great joy which it has afforded me grow cool. That joy comes too from knowing you in the immediate entourage of General de Gaulle, a man who by magnetism, wisdom and amazing actions has triumphed over all opposition. It is the great good fortune (one might say "Providence") of France to have been succored and guided by a man of such incontestable value. Even Saint-

Exupéry, at first so stubborn in his refusal, had to recognize it. I enjoyed—and felt I was doing my duty—saying so in an article on Saint-Ex that I just mailed to *Figaro*. I'm afraid I've put myself a little in his bad graces (the General's), the one time I was permitted to have a private talk with him, by attempting, and very clumsily, the defense of Maurois. But how happy it makes me to have written in my *Journal* for the 24th of June, 1940: "How could anyone refuse to agree with the Declaration of General de Gaulle?"—a passage which Aragon has studiously avoided. And since that date my feeling has only grown stronger as it found itself more and more clearly confirmed.

It will be such a pleasure to see you again, my dear Claude, so little changed, I believe, in spite of what you say, but having justified the great hopes I placed in you. But you are right: I will wait until the temperature (physical, moral, or intellectual) is more clement before I return to Paris. I admire and love your father the more for daring to assume a role which passions unchained render so dangerous. With what emotions we read his articles here, those at least which we can get our hands on, as we deplore the imperfection of the distribution of Paris papers here—often simply nonexistent. The day that the post office will allow the regular transmission of printed matter to Algiers—or any place in North Africa —will be blessed.

How sure I am of the constancy of your affection, my dear Claude! Believe me, feel me to be with you with all my heart and mind. I embrace you in friendship.

André Gide.

P.S. What's become of your friend Davray?

After that I pick up Gide's scent in my journal—how much diminished, how much sadder!

Paris, Wednesday / June 27, 1945

The other night while looking up a reference I needed in past volumes of my journal, I reread long passages written during those forgotten days, especially the Summer of 1939 with André Gide. I was surprised at how many details had slipped my mind, details which must have meant a great deal at the time, and even more surprised to realize how completely detached from Gide I am today after having loved him so dearly. My disaffection goes so far as to have prevented my attempting to see him, although I've known him to be in Paris for several months, contenting myself with just a sign of life: I sent him an autographed copy of my *Cocteau*. He failed to respond, which is rather a surprise, knowing him, but even more extraordinary that I feel no desire to see him, more than that: that such an eventuality revolts me. For me it has been as though death separated us in 1940. I can recall his tears the night of the mobilization when we bade each other farewell. I can recall his letters written during the Phony War and then the anxiety he felt on my behalf during the *Débâcle.** I deny none of that friendship which will remain one of the most precious that I have experienced. I can only observe that it finds no echo any longer in my heart.

Paris, Wednesday / July 4, 1945

Went last night with my father to the Comédie Française where the Old Vic presented *Richard III*. Before the

* The invasion of France by the Germans in May, 1940. *Trans. note.*

curtain went up I caught sight of Gide in the balcony next to his daughter, Catherine; André Gide, whom I hadn't seen since 1939. André Gide who, already seventy then, must be a very old man now . . . But never before has he looked so young—it isn't enough to say he looks no older . . . Later my father told him, "Gide, they chose a really durable wood to carve you from . . ." I admitted the other day how little pressure I felt to see him again. The emotion that overwhelmed me when I did, taught me that it was out of a kind of timidity, better, of piety, that I put off seeing him again. I feared unconsciously that after so many years we would either one of us be clumsy or cold, something which would have poisoned so many beautiful memories. But when I dashed to meet him after a far-away exchange of greetings over the noisy and indifferent public, when I found that dear forgotten face and the courtliness of his welcome, and the rather complicated delicacy of his behavior, and reciprocal and charming embarrassment of our relations as always, I have to admit (with what joy!) that neither he nor I has anything we regret in our common past. It turns out that, stung by remorse, I had written him a short letter the night before in which with great affection I had deplored our silence and this separation since his return, while putting the blame on him, inexact though it be. And it turned out that he was carrying around in his pocket last night (and he pulled it out) my book on Cocteau, which had arrived the day he returned to Paris. He swears to me he didn't see that part of the dedication which gave him my telephone number, and doubtless his conscience is no cleaner than

226

mine. The important thing is that we found each other and that we found our friendship intact.

"I believed also that you did not wish to see me." Thus André Gide affects a misunderstanding, possibly making it up as he goes along, one which puts our friendship right back on the fairly difficult terrain it occupied in the past. That first renewed contact took place in the empty corridors during the long and final ringing of the bells that announce the imminent raising of the curtain. We separated only after mutual assurances of speedily getting in touch again.

After I had rejoined my father in our seats in the orchestra, where the eternal faces of Paris society were recognizable among the sell-out audience, I looked up to where Gide sat in the balcony: he was twisted to one side and kept this awkward position just to allow a photographer to work more easily, not, however, to take his picture, but rather that of the English Ambassador's wife, Lady Diana Cooper and her party, among whom Jean Cocteau sat enthroned.

During the intermission Jacques Duchesne, whose name Radio London had made a household word, insisted that Gide and my father go backstage to meet Laurence Olivier. Duchesne insisted that it would be a good idea for two great French writers to pay their respects to a great English actor. But they were received rather coldly by the actor, almost nude, and never absolutely certain who these gentlemen were who wanted to see him. It was certainly mishandled by Duschesne, and my father is right to complain about this sort of behavior on the part of those Frenchmen who are so crazy

about England that they resemble not a little our col-
laborationists of a few months ago vis-à-vis the Third
Reich.

Paris, Saturday / July 7, 1945

Five years ago I would have piously made a point of
remembering every sentence Gide addressed to me yesterday, and commented with respect on each of these
revelations: his discovery of Latin, which he has set to
work relearning, with patience to the point of devoting
four or five hours to it each day while he was in Algiers;
that he was incapable the other night of catching a single word in spite of his perfect knowledge of English
(out of books, all of it) because of "that Chinese those
British actors mouth"; his "swan song," a work he believes "very important" . . .

I will only note that there was only one moment of
emotion in that whole evening (besides the emotion
provoked by the discovery that our friendship was
dead); a single moment during which our friendship
did come to life again, only as a memory, it is true, but
for an instant given real life, and that was when he
recalled those days we spent together in 1939: "There
are great stretches of my life that I have completely lost
track of unless someone leads me through them, while
Malagar, Pontigny, Chitré are present always in their
smallest details . . . And Brantôme! Do you recall our
lunch in Brantôme? Monsieur Gyps! You won't forget,

will you?" At that moment and only then did he have the good old smile I remember, just as I'd seen it again in the corridors of the Comédie Française.

Five years of silence create a gulf between two people. The other night I believed Gide so little changed (and my own feeling for him so much as it used to be) because we hadn't time to say anything much to one another. During those few seconds at the Comédie Française time ceased to matter, and that allowed us to enjoy for one last time the complicity and perfect understanding of a friendship which, though dead, still warmed us with its last embers.

Thus I have spent an evening with André Gide. I had invited him to dinner at the Interallié. From the first second, thanks to the unpleasant quality of our silence, I knew that it was all up with us. For a while I was still able to believe and hope that this was nothing more than the difficulty natural after so long a separation. As we walked along the Place de la Concorde I said that he had doubtless felt awe and delight on seeing again our beloved Paris. "At about the same time that I left you I left myself too," he answered, "and nothing happens to me any longer which really touches me. Seeing Paris again did not move me as I'd expected, although I found her beauty more perfect than I had remembered."

In the sumptuous dining room of the Maison des Alliés where the meager regulation dinner was served us, it became clear that I must abandon every hope of ever reviving our friendship. Quickly enough misunderstandings arose, hardly put into words, hardly noted, but perceptible somehow to both of us. We were no longer in step; our passwords were no longer the same;

229

our discordant minds were incapable of harmonizing. On the subject of my book on Cocteau he told me that the last section, with its reflections on sincerity, which would have still had interest for him in 1939, no longer meant a thing to him. And then he began praising men of action and most of all "a heroic aviator" whom he knows (Jules Roy?). He can not even suspect how familiar I am with these nostalgic admirations myself, but since I expressed certain reservations (certainly not applicable in the case of Jules Roy!) about the value of action separated from thought (as it is rare that the two are found equal in one man), I could feel him close up, suspicious and perhaps even hostile. Between us are five years of Occupation and the preoccupations that were ours, actions and inactions. But most of all I've grown up, and therefore lack interest in his eyes.

The only slight relaxation of our defenses came when we left these personal matters to talk of problems of less importance. Cocteau for instance, and Aragon, and of his *Journal,* Gide's, with the bad press it got in some quarters . . . On each of these subjects there was no question of our trying to hurt each other; but there was an equal deficiency of coming to an agreement, much less of arriving at affection.

I had a chance, however, with regard to that *Journal* of his, continued and published, to make him ashamed of having cast aspersions on introspection—it was all words, a pose. "It is possibly true," he admitted, "that I have not so completely taken leave of myself . . ."

He was happy to make use of my car to go over to Valéry's for news. François met us in the house in the Rue de
Villejust and began immediately to speak of his father's
illness, in detail and at length, as though he were describing his own sufferings. Mme. Valéry came in, exhausted and over-excited, and spoke with a volubility
that hurt us with its pretended casualness. I was alone
during the time Gide was allowed in the sickroom
where Paul Valéry was perhaps living his last hours. My
father, who had paid a call the same day, described it
to me: small, over-decorated, suffocating, and on that
narrow bed a man almost dead, his face magnificent but
tortured. A few far-away coughs which are not always
those of Gide; the voice of Mme. Valéry's sister who is
sick in the next room; an empty wicker cradle; night
falling among the trees in the courtyard; Duhamel's
dedication on the first page of a children's book: *À Paul
Valéry, le plus sérieusement du monde* . . . François
reappears, his diaphanous mask more livid than usual:
"It is disgusting to see him suffer like that . . . And his
suffering seems as intolerable to him, revolting . . . It
appears unjust and stupid . . . And it's true that, delicate
as he has always been, he has never before been really
ill . . . And it's also true that he has not said all he has to
say and that what is happening to him now *is* unjust . . ."

Gide comes back, his face somber. He is unable to
hide from François or his mother the formidable impression that their short conversation has had on him.
One thing disturbs him more than anything else: that of
all the words which the dying man had for him he was only
able to catch one or two . . . We stand around longer
than we'd have liked to, saying nothing in particular,

since Gide seemed unable to make up his mind to say good-bye. He brought up the past, this or that memory of Paul Valéry at various stages of their friendship. Mme. Valéry's stoical casualness: she tells how generously my mother has behaved in their time of trial— Paul Valéry is suppose to have said, "She just keeps thinking up ways to please me and I'm too sick to find a way to thank her"; he was so happy with some *eau de Cologne* she brought him.

As soon as we were out on the stairs Gide told me that the change which had occurred during the three days he had not seen Valéry was frightening. "He seems too far gone now to return . . ." My father said later, "He had reached that stage at which death cannot fail to be noticed in the face . . ." In my car Gide spoke very little, and the few words he said between the Rue de Villejust and the Rue Vaneau were very low and separated by great silences; all touched on the imminent death of this old friend who was his contemporary. Realizing himself to be ineluctably brought to bay by the tragic solitude of those hours preceding the final agony, it is probable that Gide was thinking more of himself than of his friend. At least my own reflections followed those lines.

Vémars, Sunday / July 22, 1945

In the old days I would have told every detail of this story, with an evil pleasure: Gide came to see me in my office, Rue Saint-Dominique, and while insisting on the devotion to duty which drives him to take up so much of his time with solicitude for an unknown correspondent, still showed delight (!) in the special nature of this business; nor would I have left out the commentary at once embarrassed and shameless with which my visitor embellished this tale. Indeed, I can do no better than quote from the letter he had had typed out for my benefit, and brought with him: "I am afraid I can not personally do anything more, suspect as I am, and hearing already the official 'Ahah! Just the sort of case that ought to interest M. Gide . . .'" And yielding to the appeal of "a small-time police spy" to make an appeal to me, since I was beyond suspicion of having personal motives for "attempting to snatch this poor creature from prison." Gide left no stone unturned in explaining, orally, his difficult position in their business: "You will understand, won't you, why I am the last person who can come to the defense of this poor young man who has been the victim, like so many, of a small-time crook, and the victim as well of an irrepressible compulsion . . ." But I have already said too much!

I did see him again, and under even more pitiful circumstances. It was the day before yesterday, in the morning. I was in the office of Gaston Palewski, where our regular conference was going on, when my secretary came after me with "urgent business." It was a telephone call from Gide, letting me know that Paul Valéry was dying, and could he have the use of my car to go see him.

A few minutes later I picked him up in the Rue Vaneau. The front door of the apartment in the Rue de Villejust was half open: we entered the silence of empty rooms. With a slow sweep of the arm Gide pointed out a sprig of boxwood in a saucer—I had noticed it too at once. He shook his head a few times, lifted his arms and said, "Bad sign, bad sign . . ." in such a strange, sad way. Then he disappeared into the next room. François walked in; his face, the first movement of his hand, and the word which followed told me everything. Paul Valéry had been dead half an hour when we got there.

I stayed there a long time, standing alone in the middle of the room. In the gloom of rooms I had never visited I could make out the pale reflections of mirrors and furtive silhouettes . . . Gide came back, his face covered with tears; there were a few more muffled condolences; then he motioned to me and we left. Downstairs, just inside the front door, the concierge and a servant were in tears. Gide had to exchange a few words with them. One of these women (not without complacency, perhaps) mentioned "his poor marine cemetery."

In the car Gide said, "No one knows anything of that man but his intellect, and believes that is all there was to know, but he was goodness itself . . ." And again he called up that pitiful scene he witnessed during his next-to-last visit, that flood of confidences meant for him alone but unintelligible. "But I don't believe it was any message for me really. He was just showing his affection, I imagine . . ."

That day I rediscovered André Gide. I mean that, for the first time since his return, I really saw him again, saw that dear face that had been forgotten so long that having it again before my eyes I did not recognize it. At the same time his voice, his mind, his heart came back to life, and perhaps my old affection.

I was never to see him again, except for one time, from afar, on the evening of the first performance of his play, the *Caves du Vatican* at the Comédie Française, December 13, 1950, a few months before his death.